W9-BLR-797

SHOW, DON'T TELL

Books by William Noble

Bookbanning in America, Middlebury, Vermont, 1990
Make That Scene, Middlebury, Vermont, 1988
"Shut Up!" He Explained, Middlebury, Vermont, 1987
Steal This Plot (with June Noble), Middlebury, Vermont, 1985
The Psychiatric Fix (with June Noble), New York, 1981
The Private Me (with June Noble), New York, 1980
How to Live With Other People's Children
   (with June Noble), New York, 1978
The Custody Trap (with June Noble), New York, 1975

Show, Don't Tell

A Writer's Guide

by William Noble

Paul S. Eriksson

PUBLISHER

MIDDLEBURY, VERMONT 05753

Manufactured in the United States of America

10 9 8 7 6 5 4 3 2 1

Library of Congress Cataloging-in-Publication Data

Noble, William.
    Show, don't tell: a writer's guide/by William Noble.
        p.   cm.
    Includes bibliographical references.
    ISBN 0-8397-7766-3
    I. Title.
  PN3355.N63   1991
  808'.02--dc20   91-16580
                                                CIP

For Madeline, from her grandfather

Contents

Preface

How difficult it can be—sometimes—to find the title for a book. Ernest Hemingway would peruse The Bible as well as William Shakespeare—arduously—in his quest for the perfect fit, and we can forgive him those occasions when simplicity and clarity gave way to a higher-minded metaphysics (such as with *Across the River and Into the Trees*). But Hemingway's titles were usually models of unpretentiousness. *For Whom the Bell Tolls* . . . *The Old Man and the Sea* . . . *The Sun Also Rises* . . . *A Farewell to Arms* . . . these offer a thumbnail of what will greet the reader between the covers, and they strike a respondent chord. The record, however, has never shown the precise length to which Hemingway went to come up with his titles, except that we know *where* he looked, and his searches must have gone on for some time.

Probably, he never had a publisher like mine.

"I've got a title for your next book," my publisher said one day. "It came to me last night while I was sleeping."

This ought to be good, I thought.

"Show, don't tell," he said.

"You mean kindergarten 'show and tell,' first grade 'show and tell'?"

No title had ever come to me while I was sleeping (though, to be fair, I did come up with one while I was in the shower). "Another book for writers, is that it?" I asked.

"An *important* book for writers," he said. "You'd be amazed how many manuscripts come in with all telling and no showing. The great majority, in fact. Writers need help in learning how to develop word-pictures for readers."

He had a point, I thought.

"Good title, isn't it?" he beamed.

My thoughts spun off for a moment. Next time maybe he'd think of a title while he was fly fishing. I wondered if he could top himself.

"Good title," I admitted.

There are a lot of adjectives to describe writing which touches the reader and creates a word-picture: vigorous, vivid, sensuous, sentimental, challenging. Writing like this brings a story to life, and there is a singular reason for it. The writer has injected drama, he or she has made things happen and has tickled the imagination of the reader.

This is what *Show, Don't Tell* is about. It offers techniques in scene development and character portrayal so readers can become part of the story that unfolds before them. There's no mystery in all of this, only a readjustment of approach so as to bring out the dramatic side of any incident or circumstance. As writers, that's what we're *supposed* to do. We think in terms of storyline and characters and scenes and moods, and these things have impact when they develop with drama. We must never be far from the drama trough because this is where we get the food for "showing" instead of "telling."

Why show and not tell? By and large, readers pick up a book to be entertained, and there's little entertainment value in being told what they are reading. They want to be caught up in the drama, to feel what the characters feel and to settle into the place the story puts them in. Bringing this about is where our creativity comes in, because the "showing" must come from our imaginations, not from a series of lecture notes that explain what is actually happening.

Think of a puppet show, where puppet characters bounce and cavort before an admiring audience. Imagine the creator of the show standing in front, slightly off to the side, visible to the audience but not part of the action on stage. He is explaining what's going on: "You see, the man has come home late, and his wife is upset because they promised to be at her mother's for dinner. The man doesn't want to go anywhere, and he's growing agitated as the wife begins to make demands. The man points to the door, telling her she could go alone, but she refuses, and she . . ."

"Hey! Sit down . . ." comes a shout from the audience.

"Get out of the way!"

"We want to see what's happening."

The audience makes clear they have come to see, feel, hear a show, not to have it explained to them.

"This isn't a lecture!"

Writers, like puppeteers, control what characters do and say, where it happens and why. The stage is where we do our work, and the story is what we try to develop. Standing to the side and explaining things—lecturing—is not dramatic or exciting or entertaining. It is telling and not showing, and audiences have a way of letting us know when that happens. A yawn, a sigh, diverted attention— finally no interest at all.

This book is a guide to the art of keeping the story on stage and its audience emotionally involved.

Showing, not telling, does the trick.

SHOW, DON'T TELL

1

Make That Opening "Happen"

One day when I was in my teens and wondering what it would be like to be a writer, I fell into conversation with a journalist who happened to be visiting. He and my father had grown up together, and in their own ways had pursued writing careers. My father had told him of my interest, and now he nodded at me with a half smile.

"Give you a tip from my first editor," he said.

I don't know what I expected, but I suppose it had something to do with Truth, with the unraveling of a special secret only writers divulged to one another. I recall that my heart beat a little faster and I held my breath.

"Simple," he said. "Start your copy halfway down the page."

"I—I don't think I understand," I said.

"That was my first reaction," he said. "My editor told me I'd figure it out, and it would make sense."

In time it did make sense for him, of course, and for me, as well. What my father's friend urged was that the lead to any story not be drawn out, that it be compressed to attract the reader's interest. *Start your copy halfway down the page* . . . means, simply, that when we begin a story, we should be ready to throw out the first few sentences of paragraphs in order to get things going.

And this applies to fiction, as well as nonfiction.

It's a fairly common habit to begin a story by "creeping up" on it, by acting less than decisively. Perhaps we're convinced that starting off with a bang will leave the reader wondering about those nagging little questions on motivation and history, which, of course, would answer everything! A few paragraphs to get us into the story, to set the stage, so to speak, and then we can let fly with the *real* drama.

Let me ask this: if we go to the theatre, are we interested in watching the stage crew push the set around, dabble with the lighting and arrange the curtain? We come to watch the play, don't we? What goes on before the curtain goes up, interests the producer, director and the union, not the audience. We come to be entertained.

It works the same way with the written word. All that stage-setting stuff is the responsibility of the editor and publisher, but the reader certainly has no interest in it. The reader wants to be entertained, and if the writer "creeps up" on the drama, the book will close with a thud.

Suppose we're doing a sea story; which of these openings would tug the reader?

   - It was a spring day in 1974 when Tom and I were getting ready to sail up the Sound to Block Island. We had bought the boat the year before but this was to be the longest sail we'd tried . . .
   - The cold dawn roused us from grainy sleep, and we stumbled from our bunks into the cockpit to stare at the open water of the Sound, less than a mile from the marina. The numbness we felt was more than the

cold, it was the uncertainty of our sail to Block
Island . . .

Which of these provides more drama? The first tells us
more, but does the explanation create a word picture?
Isn't it like setting a stage? We find out a number of things,
and in the classic journalistic sense we've provided a good
lead: we offer who (Tom and I), when (Spring, 1974),
where (on the Sound), why (to try a long sail) and how (in
a boat bought the year before).

But is it drama? Note what the second selection keys
on: the weather (cold), physical state (numbness), mental
state (uncertainty). There's a sense of place in here, of
course, because none of these other keys would have
meaning unless we had an idea where things were happening. There must be a foundation for feelings and emotions
to play against, but feelings and emotions are what appeal
to the reader and create a bond between writer and
reader. The first selection offers no feelings or emotions,
only a recitation of facts which provide information.
Drama comes when something happens or when something will happen, and when we have drama, we're going
to be showing instead of telling.

Novelist Phyllis Whitney put it quite well when she
wrote, "Perhaps the best and safest beginning is for the
writer to present immediately *someone interesting doing
something interesting.*" It sounds easy, but, of course, it
isn't. Yet she has it correct because her "something interesting" or "someone interesting" is really another way of
proposing dramatic effect. Readers want to read about
someone they find interesting because that, after all, is the
nature of entertainment (boring characters, whether in
books or on stage, are—well, boring, and no one is interested in following them). But even an interesting character
may be lost if he or she is set in an uninteresting situation;

so the character must also be doing something interesting. A reader is bound to get caught in the story this way.

See how Joseph Conrad does it with *Lord Jim*. Here's the opening paragraph:

> He was an inch, perhaps two, under six feet, powerfully built, and he advanced straight at you with a slight stoop of the shoulders, head forward, and a fixed from-under stare which made you think of a charging bull. His voice was deep, loud, and his manner displayed a kind of dogged self-assertion which had nothing aggressive in it. It seemed a necessity, and it was directed apparently as much at himself as at anybody else. He was spotlessly neat, apparelled in immaculate white from shoes to hat, and in various Eastern ports where he got his living as ship-chandler's water-clerk he was very popular.

Any doubt this is an interesting character? He's "powerfully built," with a "fixed from-under stare," looks like a "charging bull," has a "deep, loud" voice and wears nothing but white from head to toe. Conrad gives us only the physical description—not a depiction of his emotional state—but it's enough to intrigue a reader. In succeeding paragraphs Conrad describes his work as a water-clerk, calling it a "beautiful and humane occupation . . ."

An interesting character doing interesting things. This is the essence of showing rather than telling because it forces the reader to imagine something out of the ordinary, something memorable and to get caught up in it. The drama arises in the developing story of an interesting character doing interesting things, and an opening like this will hold the reader for pages and pages.

What's interesting, of course, will vary depending upon our own experiences and our sense of the unusual. Generally, however, the character would have to stand out in some fashion, physically or emotionally, and the things he or she does must appeal to emotion in the reader, either positively or negatively. It might be nothing but curiosity, but the reader has to be touched. For example:

- a character in a place he or she shouldn't be
- a character about to commit a crime
- a character working in an exotic setting

What this character is doing or about to do develops drama, and this attracts the reader. It becomes showing instead of telling because something is happening.

Many writers tend to open their stories with narrative because this allows information to be injected while the reader is most attentive. The writer has to create a sense of place for the reader in order to establish credibility of purpose and story. It's like the use of the description found on theatre programs: *ACT I: Josephine's home, August, 1938. . . .* Narrative beginnings provide the same sort of information, only they do it in more extended fashion. It will be Josephine's home, but we'll learn about the building, perhaps the furnishings, maybe the colors. The narrative might dwell on the history of the home, but it will also talk about Josephine and/or other characters, and we'll begin to see how they fit into the setting and locale. This develops the sense of place that allows the reader to move right into the story.

Narrative openings, however, must not be a recitation of facts solely for the purpose of giving out information. The tendency to do this arises because we want to make sure the reader *understands!* We don't want the reader to be confused or wondering, and we assume the best way to do this is by laying it all out.

Well, maybe that works with an academic treatise, but it won't work here. We're doing a story, and we've got to have drama, even if it is narrative. The key is to work on that sense of place, insert the reader into that story-opening by developing the physical surroundings and the nature of the character or characters. Narrative openings are really the best way to portray this sense of place because we're allowed to combine exposition with character development. When this happens, we have a situation where the reader can feel involved.

In Flannery O'Connor's short story, *Everything That Rises Must Converge,* we have an opening which perfectly illustrates this sense of place. Note how we come to know the woman through her by-play with her son, and how, after only one paragraph, we can understand where the story motivations are and how both characters feel about their hometown.

> Her doctor had told Julian's mother that she must lose twenty pounds on account of her blood pressure, so on Wednesday nights Julian had to take her downtown on the bus for a reducing class at the Y. The reducing class was designed for working girls over fifty, who weighed from 165 to 200 pounds. His mother was one of the slimmer ones, but she said ladies did not tell their age or weight. She would not ride the buses by herself at night since they had been integrated, and because the reducing class was one of her few pleasures, necessary for her health, and *free,* she said Julian could at least put himself out to take her, considering all she did for him. Julian did not like to consider all she did for him, but every Wednesday night he braced himself and took her.

Where's the drama here? There's tension, of course, between mother and son; Julian doesn't want to take her to her class, and she uses the age-old guilt throw to convince him to do so. But note something else: the mother doesn't want to take the bus downtown *because they are now integrated* (this story was first published in 1961). No longer are Black people required to sit in the back of the bus. Now they can sit alongside anyone, including Julian's mother. And she's frightened about it . . . and this also creates tension.

But the drama is more basic than this. Something is happening (a struggle between mother and son), and the reader senses that this will play throughout the story (which it does). We learn about the characters, too. The mother is vain, and she understands the power she has over her son. We know she's overweight and that her life is dull and uneventful. She sees racial integration in fearful terms and would rather pretend it didn't exist.

The son is dutiful and resentful, a combination which often leads to trouble down the line. We can assume from this opening that he doesn't share his mother's fears about racial integration, yet he buries his views under his sense of duty.

All of this from one single opening paragraph, and by the time we read these few lines we have a mental picture of Julian and his mother, we are caught up in the tension of the relationship and we have developed a sense of place—not the specifics of the locality so much as the way the characters deal with one another and with their own environment. Flannery O'Connor doesn't give us land-scape description or geographic facts and figures; she pro-vides an emotional stage for the characters to move about, and we are caught up because we *feel* for them.

Note the techniques she uses in this narrative opening:
   - deft characterizations (mother-son angst)
   - a menacing environment (to the mother)
   - a volatile thread (racial integration)
This is where drama comes from.

"Write viscerally," urged novelist Dorothy Salisbury Davis. "Make dialogue part of the action. Open a scene where you want to be, where something is happening . . ."

The other side of the narrative coin is dialogue, and here, certainly, drama can be developed. "Write viscerally . . ." she said, and she meant we should put an emotional spin on our words, think in terms of feelings instead of facts, produce highly charged material. Once we decide to have something happening (the same as with narrative), dialogue becomes a useful tool for such visceral writing because it can present emotions and feelings in a dramatic way. It's much easier, for example, to "show" someone's sadness through what they say than to write: *Tom felt deep sadness at the situation he was placed in* . . .

See the difference: "I'd prefer to be alone," said Tom. "I feel kind of depressed." The reader can identify here because he "hears" Tom's words instead of reading them. This is one of the things dialogue offers—it allows the words to ring in our ears as well as blossom in our minds. With narrative that's almost impossible.

Dialogue can develop a sense of drama so easily, and it is useful for opening a story. The one thing to remember, though, is that drama once established must be maintained; some writers allow the drama level of the opening dialogue to wash away after a page or two, as they retreat to narrative which then turns into dull exposition. Once the reader has been hooked, he or she expects to remain interested, and if the drama level drops precipitously after a few pages, the reader might well feel cheated and not be as patient with the writer as if the drama level had been lower to begin with.

But dialogue works well as a story-opening because it "shows" things well. See how Rita Mae Brown does it with *High Hearts,* her story of Virginia women during the Civil War. She begins on April 11, 1861, the day before Confederate troops fired on Fort Sumter, and she sets the action in the Virginia home of a young woman who is about to be married.

"Girl, my fingernails could grow an inch just waiting for you." Di-Peachy leaned in the doorway of Geneva's bedroom. "If they grow an inch, you'll work them off tomorrow." Geneva yanked a shawl out of her bureau, twirled it around her shoulders, and breezed past her oldest friend and personal property, Di-Peachy. At eighteen Geneva Chatfield was the tallest girl in Albemarle County as well as the best rider. She stood six feet in her stocking feet. Towering over Di-Peachy, who at five feet six inches enjoyed some height, Geneva banged down the stairs.

"Last one to Auntie Sin-Sin's—" Geneva was interrupted by Lutie Chalfonte Chatfield, her mother. Lutie had the metabolism of a humming bird and the nerves, too. "Calm yourself."

"Yes, mother."

Di-Peachy tiptoed up behind Geneva. Lutie flashed like a sheet of heat lightning. "You're going to be married tomorrow, and you're running around here like you're in a footrace . . ."

The dialogue establishes at least two things, and they are depicted much more dramatically than if this had been straight narrative. First we get a good sense of the close relationship between Geneva, who is white, and Di-Peachy who is black (even to the subtle needle about working off long fingernails on the wedding night), and we find out that Geneva will be married the next day. It isn't the narrative that provides these things, it's the dialogue, and the way the young women race through the house offers action in the midst of the dialogue. Remember Dorothy Salisbury Davis: . . . *make dialogue part of the action* . . . and this is what Rita Mae Brown has done.

We "hear" these two young women, and we can imaging them on the verge of giggling, as they banter and then as they race through the house. We can "hear" the mother stop them and admonish her daughter.

And we can "see" Geneva and Di-Peachy, eyes wide, chests heaving, little grins on their faces.

Opening dialogue produces drama like this. The reader can't help but get involved.

2

Use a Fraction of What You Know

One day I went to see a man who was curator of a historical-document collection. He was, also, a humanities professor at a well-known New England college and a well-established scholar. I had an idea for an article based upon some of the documents in his collection, but I knew he guarded his prerogatives jealously.

He was elderly and crusty and not at all certain about me.

"I'd like to look at materials in the _____ collection," I said, handing him a list of items I wanted to examine.

"You ever written on this subject?" he said, peering at me over his glasses.

I mentioned some of my publications.

"You have to know what you're talking about when you write about *this* collection."

I could sense it was going to be a difficult afternoon. "This will be my first piece on the collection," I admitted.

"I've been involved for fifteen years with the collection," he said. *"Fifteen years!"*

"I've read what you've written." I had, too, but it was pretty dull stuff and published in limited-circulation, special-interest magazines. What I had in mind was a publication of broader appeal, one that would reach coast to coast and attract hundreds of thousands of readers. "You're certainly the expert," I told him.

He coughed modestly. "I suppose I am," he agreed. And then he slipped into a twenty-minute monologue about the history of the collection, about how it came to be housed at his institution, about how he came to be named curator. "There isn't much about this collection I don't know," he said with pride.

"I'm sure I could use your help."

"It's a pretty specialized audience, you know; this collection isn't for the pop culture."

What I had in mind was to personalize the collection and turn it into a *story* instead of an analysis. I had already interviewed the two people who had put the collection together. How they did it was a tale of persistence and courage and detection. I had no doubt readers would be intrigued. "I'd like to see what you have," I said.

He peered at me over his glasses again and seemed to sigh. "You know how to handle valuable documents?"

"Yes," I responded.

"It isn't going to make a lot of sense—not without some study."

"I'd be happy for your help," I said again.

He pushed himself out of his chair and stood before me, glasses in hand. He held me with his sharp eyes, then he shook his head. "I don't know what you're going to find to write about. There is nothing in the collection that hasn't been covered already. Nothing new to find . . ."

But of course there was (few stories of mine have an unsatisfying ending), and within six months the article was published in a national magazine with a circulation in excess of one million. It generated letters and comments from every section of the country.

I've never forgotten that professor because he imprinted a key message on my writer's-sensitivity screen: *Never assume the last word has been written on anything!*

And never try to offer everything you know on a given subject; a fraction is all that's needed because you're providing a story, not a textbook. The professor's mistake was to assume that because he was the recognized expert (and acknowledged so by me) he knew what there was to know and that someone else could not come along with a different attitude and approach and carve out something else. I never professed to know as much as he knew about the subject, but I didn't need to know that much either. All I needed was a portion of the story and a clear sense of drama and how to reach the reader.

And it worked.

The problem with knowing too much is the tendency to make sure that others will hear it, and this leads to pontificating and ultimate boredom. Readers don't want to feel as if they are submerged in another's words; they want to be entertained! We can feel good that we know a lot about a subject, but we should be judicious about how we use what we know. *Slice off a portion only!* Focus on it, make it do the work of that body of knowledge crammed in the mind. For example:

> telling the story of anti-war sentiment in Viet Nam during the war would take volumes, but focusing on jungle night patrols and the inherent terror could make a dramatic statement; providing the complete story of publishing in America and censorship would take many pages, but offering the story of one controversial book and how it reached the public could make the same point but in more exciting fashion.

Writers sometimes fall into the trap of letting their erudition show. This is, after all, an uncertain profession, and there are times when we *need* to impress others with what we know—or at least we think we need to impress them. The truth is, unfortunately, that at times like this the only impression we'll make is a disgruntled one because the reader isn't about to stand still for a lecture. Remember this, don't forget it, SQUEEZE IT: *Readers want to be entertained!*

A number of years ago, novelist Willa Cather offered her thoughts on what she knew and what she used of her knowledge. In a letter to a national magazine she wrote: "Since I first saw the Puvis de Chavannes frescoes of the life of Saint Genevieve in my student days, I have wished that I could try something a little like that in prose; something without accent, with none of the artificial elements of composition . . . the essence of such writing is not to hold the note, not to use an incident for all there is to it— but to touch and pass on. I felt that such writing would be a delightful kind of discipline . . ."

"To touch and pass on." This was what she sought to do, not to milk her store of knowledge and spread it across the page, but to offer it "without accent, with none of the artificial elements of composition . . ." We see that she intended only to use a fraction of what she knew, that it was sufficient for developing a story and making it work. How well did she do? Well, here's a selection from her finest work, *Death Comes For the Archbishop*. The story is set in New Mexico during Spanish occupation, Father Vaillant is riding on horseback to Sante Fe and stops at the ranch of a rich Mexican landowner to perform a group marriage ceremony for the rancher's men and their women. The rancher shows the padre his two finest mules, and the padre jumps on the back of one of them and says:

"The saddle is to be my home in your country, Lujon. What an easy gait this mule has, and what a narrow back! I notice that especially. For a man with short legs, like me, it is a punishment to ride eight hours a day on a wide horse. And this I must do day after day . . ."

So the rancher, Lujon, offers him one of the mules, and the padre declines the offer, saying he could not ride such a fine mule while his bishop rides a less distinguished horse. So Lujon offers a horse, too:

"No, no," said Father Vaillant decidedly. "Having seen these mules, I want nothing else. They are the color of pearls, really! I will raise the price of marriages until I can buy this pair from you . . ."

Lujon sighed and looked away, but the padre continued:

"If I were a rich *ranchero,* like you, Manuel, I would do a splendid thing; I would furnish the two mounts that are to carry the Word of God about this heathen country, and then I would say to myself: *There go my Bishop and my Vicario, on my beautiful cream-colored mules . . .*"

The padre got the mules. Willa Cather doesn't go into deep discussion of guilt or the venality of the church or what the general attitude of the people toward their church was. She undoubtedly knew a great deal more about these relationships but she dramatizes what she knows in this one little scene, and we come to understand so many things all at once—materialism, venality, guilt by association, fear, control. And she remains true to what she has suggested she wished to do. *To touch and pass on.*

The entire scene takes no more than five pages; there's no deep exposition or further description of the relationship between Lujon and the padre. This one scene does it, yet we've learned and experienced a great deal. We know now how the church interacted with its people in New

Mexico territory many years ago and we've been entertained at the same time! The focus of a single scene.

We've got two basic decisions to make when it comes to writing about something we know well. First, we have to zero in on where the drama lies, we have to search for those exciting parts which will tug at the reader's emotions and develop a sense of identity. Not everything in the Viet Nam War, for example, was dramatic or exciting. There was much that was routine, and merely because we might know the subject well doesn't mean the readers are going to be interested in everything we know about the war, fictionalized or not. A good writer seeks out the drama, no matter the circumstances.

Second, once we've grabbed hold of the drama, we have to decide which part of it we want to work with. Many times there can be so much drama that we find ourselves with an embarrassment of riches, and we can't narrow down the storyline. What happens is that the story explodes in a number of directions, and we find our minds swirling as we try and keep control, which we never seem to manage. The story spins away from us, and we hold our heads and wonder why. The culprit, again, is that we know too much and by God! we're going to use it all.

Instead, of course, we should be seeking out those dramatic details which give us the *best* story. At times like this we need to use a stiletto and not a broad sword, because the story will live or die by the precision of our emotional appeal. Drama which has no essential relevance to our story is better left out, even though it might add an exciting footnote or provide an additional dimension. We need to stay focused, and we have to be careful and stay in control of the dramatic landscape.

Pauline Bloom believes that it's natural to want to use the interesting ideas and circumstances we uncover during research or after some hard thinking. ''Serendipity is fun,'' she says, but we have to be careful, and we should ask ourselves some hard questions about the "treasure" we've found:

- "Does [it] avert attention from the main storyline?"
- "Would removing [it] harm the story or confuse readers in any way?
- "Does [it] answer questions the reader might ask— and if the questions go unanswered, will the reader be frustrated?
- "Does [it] clarify in readers' minds who a person is or where a place is?
- "Does [it] make the story more concrete, real or credible?"

Let's see how this works. Heywood Broun was a renowned newspaper columnist in New York more than a half century ago, well known for his liberal views. His mother, however, was politically opposite, and she regularly sent scathing letters to Broun's newspaper to complain about his column. In addition, she hated unions, and in a column devoted to her, Broun described her attitude:

For one afternoon there was no elevator service in the apartment building in which my mother lives, and now it has been restored, which makes my mother pretty indignant. The service came back because the landlord signed up with the union. My mother is considering walking up and down the five flights of stairs as a protest . . .

A few paragraphs later, he wrote:

When the revolution comes, it's going to be a tough problem what to do with her. We will either have to shoot her or make her a commissar. In the meantime we still dine together.

At no time in this column does Broun describe his mother physically, nor give her age, nor mention her attitude about anything else specifically except how she feels about unions. He doesn't quote her or provide other anecdotes about her beliefs or how others feel about her. He's kept this extremely narrow, and it works. Now suppose he wanted to bring in some other anecdotes because they were amusing and would develop her character even further? Using Pauline Bloom's suggestions, he would have to weigh whether this new "treasure" averted attention from the main storyline, answered questions the reader wouldn't already have gained, added clarification about what his mother really believed, made the story more real or credible. Would removing the information harm the story or confuse the reader?

Pretty obvious what the answer would be. Heywood Broun's mother was fully dramatized by the simple description of her attitude about the elevator and the fact she wrote scathing letters to his employers. Do we need to know any more about her to gain a full appreciation? Broun, obviously, knew a great deal more about her than he told, but he limited himself, and the dramatic effect blossomed. His feelings for her were clear, too, in the last line:

In the meantime we still dine together.

Nothing more than that. A son's affectionate portrait, and she lives in his mind and ours.

All of us have been urged to keep a notebook or journal of our thoughts, impressions, character studies, sketches, poems and any other fragment of the writer's art. Developing discipline is one purpose but equally important is to get us familiar with people or places or events which we might ultimately write about. The more we jot down, goes the theory, the more familiar we'll be when it comes time to write the real thing. I have no problem with this approach, in fact, I encourage it. But it's not without its drawbacks. The tendency can be (and I know because it happened to me) to develop something so deeply in the notebook that when it comes time to write the story, all of it simply transfers—all of it! We don't pick and choose among the details we put in the story because they came from our journal, and our journal is the cookpot of our creativity. All of it seems dramatic, so in it goes.

What we should be doing is to pick and choose, using only those items which can pass the test Pauline Bloom outlined. Simply because we've come to know a great deal about a character or about a setting or about an event doesn't mean we have to use it all. Think dramatically, first . . . and then think *most* dramatically. Avoid the tendency to use everything that pops from our own creativity.

Gail Godwin shows us how to pick and choose with her short story, *The Angry Year*. The narrator is in college and a writer, working for the college newspaper and doing a column called "Without Restrictions." The narrator writes angry, sarcastic and critical comments about the campus fraternities and sororities and their customs, and one day she receives a letter from a male student who criticizes her column as unseemly and ineffective for someone who also professes a love for good literature. She's a bit dismayed but continues with her vitriol and receives a couple more letters from him continuing his criticism. One day they meet, and she discovers he is 27 years old and a Viet Nam Marine veteran. They begin to talk, and within a moment or two she tells him:

"Well, I'm an only child. But my father has this problem with his temper and keeps losing jobs. I had these war bonds, luckily, my aunt and uncle used to send me every Christmas, and I cashed them in so I could go to this measly little college in my hometown as a day student. The only reason I'm here is because I made straight A's for two years—did nothing but grind, grind, grind. Now I intend to have some fun." I was shocked at myself. I had not even told my Christian Scientist roommate the whole truth . . .

This is all we ever get about the narrator's background. She never elaborates further and she never rehashes. We find out she comes from a poor family, she had to struggle to get into college and to transfer, she feels she's missed out on a lot. All of this adds up to resentment and anger at those who might have a great deal more, such as members of fraternities and sororities. Why does she open up so quickly to this older man? She senses someone like herself, who has struggled. (He was in the Marines, don't forget, and at his age we can assume he had to make enough money elsewhere to pay for his own education.) Note the title—*The Angry Year*—and the way she plays it out.

But note, too, that her anger, which drives this story, is not overplayed and overdeveloped. In one single dialogue passage we find the entire basis for her feelings, and it's enough. The author could have told us much more about where the anger came from and about how it develops, but she doesn't. The limited description serves its purpose, and we aren't overwhelmed with details which probably wouldn't add much, and which might actually detract from the drama.

Note, too, how the author, at the end of the dialogue passage, has the narrator express shock at herself for divulging this information to someone who was barely more than a stranger. This appeal to emotion adds tension to an already interesting scene (interesting because we're learning about the narrator's background for the first time), and it shows a clear portrait of what was going through her mind at the time. A word-picture, to be sure.

3

Tension Means Conflict Means Action

Recently, I was on a writers' panel, and we talked about plotting. One panelist suggested that working chronologically had the advantage of keeping everyone in step. "You don't have to go back later and fill in details," she said. "The story has a beginning, a middle and end, and the reader understands that."

Another panelist agreed that this linear view of story-writing mirrored life itself. "All of us live chronologically," he said, "we're always *starting* at the beginning and working through to the end. Whether it's school or a relationship or a job or even a marriage. We see all these things from some beginning point and while they may not have ended, yet—eventually they will. Everything does."

But the idea of writing as a mirror to life wasn't embraced by other panelists, or by many in the audience. "Life is a good springboard," someone said, "a starting point. But we have to use our imaginations to make things more interesting."

"There are large parts of life that are really pretty dull," another said. "If we wrote the way things actually happened, without embellishment, most readers would be bored silly.''

I mentioned the one thing that most of us in that room knew was essential for story development—the presence of tension or conflict. "How many times during a day— any day—will we find ourselves in a conflict-laden situation?" I asked. "How often do we find our hackles rise or our sense of foreboding emerge?"

Most agreed times like these didn't happen frequently, yet if writing was a mirror to life and we wanted to get it all down on the page, uneventful days would have to share space with the times when conflict and tension would be present. "In short," I said, "writing which mirrors life in all respects is writing which will turn readers off. No one wants to wade through all the dull stuff to reach the little gems that might turn them on. Our daily lives are not a chronicle of excitement—they are a chronological exercise in moving from beginning to end.''

Some thought my attitude cynical, but the point I was trying to make was that writing is not a mirror that picks up every facet of our lives; it is a telescope which focuses on certain experiences and then molds them. Writing picks and chooses from life just as the person who is watching his or her weight picks and chooses from the buffet table.

The idea of tension and conflict is precisely the sort of thing the writer must pick and choose for his story. Once in a while I teach writing to fifth and sixth graders, and I always start them off with a small exercise in developing tension. "Write down three things you like," I tell them and then I suggest they pick one. "Now write me a paragraph about what you've chosen," I say. When they finish, I tell them to write down three things they *don't* like, and then I say, "Now choose one of the three and write me a paragraph about *that*." When they finish, I tell them, "Now write me two paragraphs about what you like and what you don't like and tell me a story about it; connect your like and dislike."

And the stories come flowing out. The reason? They have built-in tension between the item they liked and the item they didn't like, and by trying to work them together, they have developed natural conflict.

It isn't a mirror to life, certainly, but it does focus on something of interest—the drama inherent in any conflict situation. Because tension is conflict (or as one well-known editor put it, tension is confrontation, either internal or external), and when we have conflict, we have action . . . and when we have action, we have something happening . . .

And when something is happening, we have an opportunity to *show* the reader.

Take the way it operates with characterization. Tension is essential for effective character portrayal. As writer Michael Newton puts it:

"Tension . . . should arise naturally from complications your characters confront en route to solving a problem. There are varieties of tension, and they don't all hinge on a threat to life or limb. There may be tension in the interaction of your characters, beyond the root antagonisms of the story—suspicions of motives, for example, or extreme differences in politics or education . . ."

As with most other writing techniques tension can be shown or told, but it is certainly more effective when it is shown. See the difference:

Jed and Ted were alike in so many ways, as twins usually are. But when it came to politics, they diverged, sometimes violently. Jed was the liberal, and he never understood Ted's support of capital-gains taxes or social program cut-backs. Hadn't their father been a Kennedy family staffer?

And now this:

"Materialist!" Jed shouted at his brother.

"Capitalist!"

Ted smiled benignly; he'd heard most of it before. "You'd give away the store," he said.

"Doesn't it bother you millions of Americans go hungry everyday? Only a concerned government can help."

"Too much government already," Ted said.

"Let's give money to the people who can *do* things."

"Dad would be embarrassed to hear you . . ."

"Dad would probably agree with me now . . ."

The second portion portrays the disagreement between the brothers more vividly than does the first portion. By using dialogue we can highlight the conflict and the tension and provide it with more drama. If we added a couple of gestures for Jed or Ted, if we had their faces darken or flush, if we had their words become clipped or growled, the drama would intensify. These are the sort of embellishments that wouldn't work with narrative (or at least not well; I suppose we could write that their arguments occasionally ended with flushed faces or clipped words, but the results seem tame compared to the actual dialogue). They *do* work with dialogue, however, and we have a strong word-picture as a result.

Effective tension can also arise even if the conflict is seen in the mind of only one character, that is, if the other character isn't aware of it. Tension doesn't have to be a two-way street, so long as the necessary element of confrontation exists. Sometimes this type of tension actually begins inside the mind of one character where there is an internal value conflict (think of anyone wrestling with a major decision). The character's attention then shifts toward a second character, but the second character could be oblivious to the first character's attention and internal conflict. Such is the way novelist Anne Tolstoi Wallach in *Women's Work* portrayed her protagonist, Domina Drexler, who is a vice-president of a New York advertising agency but who wants to move higher. She sees herself unfairly treated by Brady Godwin, the head of the agency, and she writes him a memo (note Domina's internal conflict and the way she fixes it on Brady Godwin):

> Memo to Brady Godwin. It's time we talked about my promotion. For two years I have handled every problem, built up every product, charmed every client of this agency. I have surpassed everyone's expectations of a mere woman. I am never sick. I get to meetings absolutely on time. I am always calm and even-tempered. The fact that I go home and cry is unknown to you, and cannot be used against me. I am talented, attractive, steady. People who work for me respect, admire and even like me.
>
> Every single person in the office who does the kind of work I do is already a senior vice-president . . .

The confrontation is still in her mind, but tension oozes from the story. Now look at the technique this author uses: a memo, not straight narrative, not dialogue, a simple descriptive device which serves the purpose of portraying the conflict. By using the memo device she also provides the underlying theme for the book which is sex discrimination in the executive suite. Yet note this: at no point does she refer to "sex discrimination" or have the characters discuss it. The memo describes it in personal terms, in what its impact has been on Domina Drexler, and we sure do get the message.

And because of the personal nature of the memo, the author has given us more showing than telling. If she has described the sex discrimination in less personal terms (third person, for instance: "Domina felt . . . ," "Domina thought . . ." "She wanted . . ."), the word-picture would have been less vivid and the event less marked.

But she didn't, and it isn't.

When we examine what goes into tension and conflict, we find the presence of contrast, a sense of difference and diversity. The contrast might be little more than two different hair styles, or it might be as momentous as the struggle between good and evil. But contrast is what fuels the idea of tension and conflict because it sets the agenda of opposition.

For example, one character would be blond and open and vivacious and spontaneous . . .

Another character would be dark haired and brooding and quiet and studied.

The contrasts between these characters is obvious, yet until we put them on the page they have no conflict. Merely because one is blond and the other dark haired doesn't—*automatically*—mean there will be conflict between them. We have to work up the conflict, but we have an advantage because we set up the contrasts. Now we can insert them both into our work, and their contrasts in looks and attitudes will ignite tension, should we wish to develop it. It could go something like this:

> She glanced at the quiet, dark haired man in the corner. He never, *ever* joined the laughter at the main table, content to immerse himself in one of her father's books. He looked . . . interesting, she wondered what his voice would sound like.
>
> "I'm Amy," she said, holding out her hand.
>
> He looked up and nodded. "I know," he said, returning to his book.
>
> "Hey!" she said, picking the book from his hands. "You have a name . . . ?"

The contrasts in these characters get us going, and the tension begins to flow. Soon, the essential differences in their characterizations will merge into a complete story line, and we'll come to know them and to expect them to react and say things in certain ways.

Novelist Nancy Kress sees contrast as adding reader interest, especially at the beginning of a story. It "make[s] a story opening arresting enough to give you time to build narrative tension . . ." she says. "You create [tension through contrast] by juxtaposing two elements that at first seem very different, perhaps even direct opposites. Like the pull on the opposite sides of a clothesline, the pull of these contrasting elements creates tension."

She's right, of course. Look no further than the story of *Romeo and Juliet* where two young people from families which hate one another could somehow fall in love. When the lovers first meet, the clothesline couldn't be more taut; this is the contrast, the two families in deepest conflict. Then, as the story builds, the tension of their romance takes over, and the drama grows.

Remember, contrast is merely the opening step in developing tension and conflict. "Few books will use contrast as an overall organizing principal," adds Nancy Kress. "But many incorporate it in minor incidents."

A first step, but an important one.

Now let's enlarge on contrast, let's go beyond character or physical description, and think in terms of plot or story line. Take a standardized circumstance, such as a birthday party, and invert the facts. When we think of a birthday party, we think of joy and happiness and celebration. But suppose at *this* birthday party we have anger and humiliation and confrontation. This is the contrast; how we play it out is the tension we'll develop for our story. What we've done is to take a situation and instead of allowing the usual reactions to take place, we've turned them inside out, we've inverted them, so that *unusual* reactions take place. The drama is heightened, and the reader will pay close attention because it isn't quite what he or she expected.

This contrast within a situation can be played out in any number of ways: a loving family that shares a dark secret, a medical story that reeks of self-interest, greed and un- kindness, a story of ambition that fails, again and again.

Or how about a crime story that bursts with humor? A kidnapping, for example, that ends up toasting the kidnap- pers. This is what O Henry did in his well-known *The Ransom of Red Chief*. Two kidnappers take the young son of a prominent citizen and hold him in a cave in the mountains outside town. The boy turns out to think of it as an adventure, just like camping out, and he gives him- self the name, Red Chief, the Indian. The kidnappers send the ransom note, but Red Chief tells them he doesn't want to go home, and they begin to wonder about their scheme when they discover that no one is searching for the boy. In the meantime Red Chief is bedeviling the kidnappers, tying them up when they sleep, pretending to scalp them with a real knife and generally turning their quiet exis- tence into a maelstrom. After a sleepless night and no response from their ransom note, the kidnappers discuss what to do next:

> Just then we heard a kind of war-whoop, such as David might have emitted when he knocked out the champion Goliath. It was a sling that Red Chief had pulled out of his pocket, and he was whirling it around his head.
>
> I dodged and heard a heavy thud and a kind of sigh from Bill, like a horse gives out when you take his saddle off. A niggerhead rock the size of an egg had caught Bill just behind his left ear. He loosened him- self all over and fell in the fire across the frying pan of

hot water for washing dishes. I dragged him out and poured cold water on his head for half an hour . . .

Red Chief makes it so miserable for his kidnappers that they finally write to his father and offer to *pay* to give Red Chief back. The father graciously assents, and the kidnappers take off across the state line.

Here, then, is a situation with an unusual twist. There's a crime, but it turns out to be hilarious, not forbidding or fearful. It is the contrast between what we come to expect from a crime story (violence and frightening events) and what really takes place (which skewers our expectations) that creates the interest and the drama. Actually, there is double tension here: there is the kidnapping, which under usual circumstances is a serious, dangerous crime; and there is the concern about whether the kidnappers will be safe from Red Chief. The kidnapping, itself, becomes ludicrous when we see how Red Chief has manhandled the kidnappers, and so the tension here is neutralized. But the other tension—will the kidnappers be safe?—plays out to the end of the story, and because it is such an unusual twist (something like "man bites dog") the reader stays with it all the way.

Because the reader wants to know the answers, too. Who wins, Red Chief, the kidnappers, or Red Chief's father?

I put my money on the father. He's the only one who made a profit.

There's little doubt that if O. Henry had written this story without the humor and had played it as a straight kidnapping without the convoluted circumstances, much more would have been needed. It is the contrast which gives it depth and which allows the characters to develop. Try imagining the story with a scared, weepy, uncertain young boy in the place of Red Chief. Unless we change all the other characters, too, the story will fall flat. What gives the story pizazz, and what holds our interest, is the reversal in circumstances, and the contrast that creates.

What gets us involved is the tension that flows from the contrasts. Creating that tension is what builds drama and excitement.

And now we're showing and not telling.

4

Create a Sense of Immediacy

One of the most useful pieces of writing advice I ever received came from my first editor, when I was struggling to develop television-news-writing skills. "Write about people," he said, "don't write about things. The audience wants stories, not lectures."

What he meant was that the audience needed to feel involved, to be close to what was happening, and stories about people make that possible. Why? Because the audience can participate and enter the scene.

We call this creating a *sense of immediacy*. It's a fine tool for showing instead of telling.

Some years ago the famed broadcast journalist, Edward R. Murrow, and his well-known producer, Fred W. Friendly, developed a series of programs for radio, "Hear it Now!" and for television, "See it Now!." They took well-known events from history and re-created interviews, eye-witness accounts, personal agonies and triumphs. By understating both the tension and the suspense, they placed the listener or the viewer right in the middle of what was happening. *You are there!* shouted the radio and television signal.

And the audience felt every nuance.

What Murrow and Friendly did was to create a sense of immediacy for their audience, and they did it by focusing their stories on people and their feelings and reactions. NOW! THIS VERY MOMENT!

You are there!

As writers we need to do the same thing—we must develop that sense of immediacy in our readers. Janet Burroway, in her fine book, *Writing Fiction,* tells us that we have to ". . . focus attention, not on the words, which are inert, nor on the thoughts these words produce, but through these to felt experience, where the vitality of understanding lies." The reader must become involved, must *feel* what is happening on the pages.

Put it another way: a physics teacher stands before a class and lectures for half an hour on the basic theory of relativity, $E = MC^2$. (Energy equals mass times the speed of light squared). He explains and explains . . .

And the students struggle to grasp the abstraction.

Another physics teacher rejects the lecture approach. "Watch this!" he says, taking a large metal ball and rolling it down a set of tracks where it trips light switches at an increasing rate, which, in turn, operates a gear box at the back of the room.

See? says the teacher. *See it now!*

Lecture versus demonstration. Which fires the audience attention span?

Show, don't tell, and the students are part of it. Translate this to the written page, and we have the necessary drama and impact. The immediacy of the demonstration is what draws the audience in and rivets their attention. They are participants.

We can write this way, too. *You are there!* is the key, and writing techniques will establish it. When we strive for immediacy, most of us tend to think in the present, that is, what is happening to us, or to our characters, now, today. And that's fine because creating a sense of immediacy is often hinged on developing something we can touch easily, on developing a familiar reality.

For example, there's no denying we live in a technological world, and we're familiar with exotic names for exotic equipment and with the outlandish things some of that equipment can accomplish, especially in a military context. We may not understand how it works, but we do understand it exists, and we're awed by what it can do. Tom Clancy understands this too, and in his book, *Clear and Present Danger,* he shows us the dramatic possibilities with techno-language and how it can create a sense of immediacy. This is a story of a struggle with the Colombian drug cartel, and Clancy sets up a meeting at the Bogota, Colombia airport between Colombian officials, the FBI Director and the DEA Administrator. He describes the Americans' arrival this way:

> The VCA-20A, the military version of the G-III executive jet, flew in with a commercial setting on its radar transponder, landing at 5:39 in the afternoon at El Dorado International Airport, about eight miles outside Bogota. Unlike most of the VCA-20As belonging to the 89th Military Airlift Wing at Andrews Air Force Base, Maryland, this one was specially modified to fly into high-threat areas and carried jamming gear originally invented by the Israelis to counter surface-to-air missiles in the hands of terrorists or businessmen . . .

He achieves immediacy by referring to the military equipment, not by lengthy description, but by techno-phrasing ("VCA-20A" "G-III"), and he doesn't bother to describe exactly what those shorthand designations mean. But he doesn't have to because we're used to reading about, to using (especially if we have been in the military) such designations ourselves. It's a coding system which tells us something is official and probably important. It's modern and familiar and that makes it immediate.

It's easy to do with fiction (and there's no rule that says we must be totally accurate—here's a place to use our imaginations):

> *a weapon*—"The SK-28 missile sat on its launch pad, its UAK nosecone swathed in blue beryllium reflector paint, its two million horsepower GE engines rumbling impatiently . . ."

> *a computer*—"The three-dimensional screen images from the LX-129 reflected onto the VI4 printer, and the black diamond stylus reproduced the shadings and the angles with uncanny accuracy . . ."

> *a vehicle*—"The MRC-160 had the speed of a grand touring car and the durability of a PC40 light tank, but it also carried 'Pixie' flame throwers and the GOPHR mobile land-hugging torpedo . . ."

Need I add that any resemblance to weapons, computers or vehicles used anywhere in the world is purely coincidental?

There's more that Tom Clancy does, too. Note how he weaves in current circumstances to keep the immediacy level high. He refers to terrorists, surface-to-air missiles and the military skill of the Israelis, all things which pulsate from the front pages. These strike a familiar chord with the reader, and they keep Tom Clancy's story fresh. Nothing is remote, nothing is esoteric, everything is right in front of the reader, as immediate as today's news. Clancy's use of techno-words and techno-phrasing along with his contemporary references develops a vivid sense of immediacy. The reader is *there!* No doubt about it.

Sometimes, of course, seeking that contemporary "hook" can be taken to outrageous lengths. Giving the reader chances to identify with the story by rolling out current references can actually negate the sense of immediacy when it's overdone. The reader doesn't need to be sprayed with reminders, only sprinkled with them. Otherwise, it will seem as if the story is little more than a vehicle for contemporary references, that the tail would seem to be wagging the dog, and when this happens, the reader will lose sight of where the story is going because he or she will be distracted by the references.

This is what happened with Brett Easton Ellis's controversial novel, *American Psycho,* where he portrayed a serial killer and described most graphically what the killer did to his victims. The story was tough going for the reader—a far cry from the conventional novel, mainly because the characters were unlikable and the descriptions ludicrous and often disgusting. Even tougher because of the author's obsession with displaying the trappings of modern life. To stretch a familiar phrase: he never saw a brand-name he didn't like. Here's a sample:

> He continues talking as he opens his new Tumi calfskin attaché case he bought at D.F. Sanders. He places the Walkman in the case alongside a Panasonic wallet-size cordless portable folding Easa-phone . . . After I change into Ralph Lauren monogrammed boxer shorts and a Fair Isle sweater and slide into silk polkadot Enrico Hidolin slippers . . . The shoes I'm wearing are crocodile loafers by A. Testoni . . . He's wearing a linen suit by Canali Milano, a cotton shirt by Ike Behar, a silk tie by Bill Blass and cap-toed leather lace-ups from Brooks Brothers . . .

Name-brand addiction, that's what this is. On a smaller scale, with fewer references, it might work to build a sense of immediacy. But when it is indulged in with the eagerness of a chocolate-lover loose in a chocolate factory, its impact is diminished. Instead, we get caught up (if there are enough image-creating words and phrases to catch us up) in the overabundance of references, and we lose sight of what actually is happening. Like a non-chocolate-obsessed visitor at the chocolate factory we wish the tour would continue so we can learn how chocolate is made instead of stopping and obsessing when the first gobs of unmolded chocolate are trotted out.

Writing about contemporary references, whether they are things we might wear or see or hear or taste, is a fine technique for developing immediacy—so long as it's done with care. Readers need to know where they are in terms of time and space, and bringing in the occasional name-brand item is an efficient way of doing that. For example, we could write:

> He fingered the lapels of his Brooks Brothers suit, knowing its cut would stamp him with substance and certainty. He'd remembered the Countess Mara tie, too, its rich blend of azure and silver setting off the powder blue of his shirt. He wanted to make an impression . . .

There's purpose in using these brand names, and if the author doesn't go any further in describing what the character is wearing, we get a good mental image. But transpose the Brett Easton Ellis approach:

> He fingered the alferi-cut lapels of his Brooks Brothers suit, noting the late hour from his platinum-banded Philipe Patek. Marge would have the Mercedes 500 SL waiting outside, and she'd grin when she saw him in the Tripler's Egyptian-cotton shirt. So soft, she'd murmur, running aloe-creamed fingers across his chest, then caressing the silkiness of his Countess Mara tie. What an impression you'll make, she said . . .

And there's too much. We don't need all these brand name references to get the message that the character is well-to-do and conscious of fashion. The first selection does the job well enough, and we don't feel overwhelmed with brand-name references. The point to remember is that we want to develop immediacy, and that's achieved with subtlety more than crashing reality. A brand name now and then is a good device, but it ceases to be helpful when it's overused.

What, after all, is the purpose of a sense of immediacy? It's easy to talk in terms of reader identification and reader involvement, we understand how important it is to keep the reader's attention and make sure he or she feels the things that are happening on the page. But how do we translate it into practical use, how do we *do* it? Author David Madden has a few tips for us, and while some might seem obvious, it's important to remember that writing with a sense of immediacy can slide away unless we remain conscious of its need. We can become engrossed in our story to such an extent that we forget the practical side of story telling: *Is the reader involved? Am I placing the reader in the middle of things? Is the reader there?*

Madden suggests that we:

- use chronological sequence ("I had lunch, then I went to the store," not "I went to the store, having had lunch");
- stay with active verbs ("The hardworking men mined the ore," not "The ore was mined by the hardworking men");
- make transitions sharp and neat. (The quicker the better, keep the bridges short);
- emphasize through repetition (in moderation, of course) of words, phrases, sentences.

There's a certain attention-grabbing character to each of these, and that's what we're after. The object of immediacy is to bring the events on the page home to the reader in as dramatic a way as possible, and each of these suggestions accomplishes it. Take the idea of keeping things in chronological sequence. One obvious advantage is that the reader won't be confused, because all of us respond to events in order, and chronological order is the order we're most familiar with. Suppose there's a confrontation:

> I watched him lunge to grab her before she leaned on the broken railing. Her face showed surprise, then fear, then anger. He nodded an apology and stepped back and I could see her lips move rapidly, her head bobbing. He shrugged and smiled, and she glanced behind her. Then she shivered . . .

Now let's break up the chronology:

> There was surprise on her face after he grabbed her to keep her from leaning on the broken railing. I could see her lips move even though he'd already nodded an apology. When she glanced behind her, she shivered, while he was shrugging and smiling at her anger . . .

The immediacy comes through clearly in the first selection, but it's blunted in the second. Chronology offers a floor for the action, allowing matters to proceed without obstacles. The same is true with the other devices: active verbs keep the story pot bubbling; short transitions prevent a loss of attention when there's a change of scene; and repetitions force home certain images that will stay in the forefront of the reader's mind.

Remember! Remember! Remember! Active verbs bring immediacy. Keep those transitions short!

But this isn't all there is to immediacy. A savvy writer can develop a style whereby he or she talks to the reader, almost as if it's a private conversation. One obvious technique is to use the first person:

> *I told her I'd come when she whistled . . .*

It's not so intimate in the third person:

> *He told her he'd come when she whistled . . .*

Then put it all in the present tense:

> *I tell her I'll come when she whistles . . .*

And the immediacy grows. Now, if the savvy author is Raymond Carver, the late, renowned short-story writer, the sense of immediacy grows even more. In his short story, *Intimacy,* Carver has a man stopping in to see his former wife. They begin to talk about their marriage and how it turned sour, and they dredge up old hurts and angers:

> She says, Honey, no offense, but sometimes I think I could shoot you and watch you kick.
>
> She says, You can't look me in the eyes, can you?
>
> She says, and this is exactly what she says, You can't even look me in the eyes when I'm talking to you.
>
> So, okay, I look her in the eyes.
>
> She says, Right. Okay, she says. Now we're getting someplace, maybe. That's better. You can tell a lot about the person you're talking to from his eyes . . .

We have the present tense, we have the first person . . . and we have no quotation marks. There is dialogue, to be sure, *but there are no quotation marks!* Does this make any difference to the immediacy? It probably helps it along because it becomes more of a personal memo between writer and reader, a type of personal note which doesn't need the niceties of punctuation. Think about it for a moment . . . If we're communicating with a special friend and it's done in a casual manner, would we bother with the formality of punctuation? We'd assume the other would understand.

And so the immediacy (and the intimacy, too—because they are entwined, somehow) grows. But now look at what Carver has also done. He speaks to the reader *directly:*

> She says, *and this is exactly what she says* . . .

Carver is making it clear to the reader, he's emphasizing what she is saying, and he's speaking directly to the reader. There's no other purpose for the phrase because there's no one else involved in the story, only the man and his wife and the reader. And by speaking to the reader Carver has brought the idea of immediacy to a vivid form. The reader is his partner now, and that's involvement.

Speaking to the reader like this is a good technique but as with so many techniques it should not be overdone. Carver is careful with it, using it sparingly, and so the effect is substantial. But if there's an aside to the reader in almost every paragraph or even a couple times a page, the technique would lose its impact and become ineffective.

The sense of immediacy carries with it the building of intimacy between reader and writer, because both are forced to come closer to one another if the story is going to work. The reader must feel the events, and the writer must open the story up for the reader to enter. Devices such as first person and present tense are keys that will unlock the door, and then, when we add personal touches, such as no quote marks and direct reader-author dialogue, the door will swing wide open.

You are there! says the author.

I am, I am! says the reader.

5

Think Similes and Metaphors

As writers we're urged to produce something that conveys a word-picture to the reader. We're asked to wave our fingers across the keyboard and *bingo! presto!* it becomes an image cast in the reflection of our own creativity.

A picture forged from our words.

If the word-picture is what we strive to develop, then all writing is only a prelude because the word-picture is the ultimate product. Unlike the painter or the sculptor, however, we communicate more easily because words are the simplest and most customary form of idea exchange. Many of us don't know how to paint or sculpt, but all of us know how to write *something* that says something. We know how to get an idea across with words, even as we profess ignorance over how to do it on canvas or with clay.

The key is to think in terms of that ages-old academic concept—compare and contrast. Compare this with that . . . contrast that with this . . . What this accomplishes is to develop a word-picture by forcing us to think in images. If we must think of one thing by comparing it to another—a mountain configuration in the shape of an elephant's head and back, for instance—we present the image so the reader can see it in his or her mind. Instead of writing that the mountain had large humps and dips, we call in the elephant image, and the reader can imagine it more easily. The word-picture forms.

Comparing and contrasting images is what similes and metaphors do, and the purpose is to build up that word-picture and clarify it. To show it, not tell it.

First, a couple of definitions: similes and metaphors both compare or contrast images, but *similes* do so with the use of the word *like* or *as*. Her hair smelled *like* fresh roses . . . His eyes were *as* hard, black stones. Metaphors designate one object that is used to suggest another. The out-of-control car was a roaring beast, chasing through the infield, devouring any who got in its way. There's a symbolism in the metaphor which doesn't occur in similes, because a metaphor changes the character of the underlying object while the simile keeps it the same. Thus, a ship could be as sleek as a confident young woman yet remain a ship (simile), while a ship could *be* a young woman, headstrong, energetic, graceful, and become the character (metaphor).

Creating the word-picture *is* the writer's art (the metaphor), it's not *like* the painter's or sculptor's art (the simile). We do understand the idea of a word-picture, we can visualize it, almost as if it's a dialogue bubble right from a cartoon—*bingo! presto!* the word-picture materializes and becomes what we want it to become.

And so we go back to comparing and contrasting. It's easier with similes because the simile by its nature compares one thing (or one person) with another. Yet the metaphor compares, as well, in the sense that it shows how certain characteristics of one thing can make it into something else. It isn't *like* that something else, it *is* that something else.

In the hands of a writer like William Faulkner, a metaphor can be handled deftly. Here's what he does in his novel, *Light in August,* where he describes a sign on the front lawn of Reverend Gail Hightower's house in the small town of Jefferson, Mississippi. Hightower had offended and embarrassed the people in town to such an extent that they stopped coming to his church, and he finally left the ministry. His sign now advertises that he is offering art lessons, handpainted Christmas and anniversary cards and photographic developing.

From the window he can also see the sign, which he calls his monument. It is planted in the corner of the yard, low, facing the street. It is three feet long and eighteen inches high—a neat oblong presenting its face to who passes and its back to him. But he does not need to read it because he made the sign with hammer and saw, neatly, and he painted the legend which it bears, neatly too, tediously, when he realized that he would have to begin to have money for bread and fire and clothing . . .

The remainder of the chapter goes into why the sign is his monument, his epitaph, the story of his life. The sign becomes a metaphor for the way Reverend Gail Hightower has lived, and the image called up is of a monument, not a sign at all. Doesn't the metaphor create a word-picture, so we see the sign really describing what has become of Hightower's life? How disgraced can a minister become if he is reduced to—giving art lessons, selling greeting cards, developing film?

And the sign on his lawn becomes a tombstone for what he used to be.

Faulkner's use of metaphor here makes the word-picture more effective because the image is clear and symbolic. We understand what he is driving at, and it's much more dramatic than if he had written:

> Reverend Gail Hightower lost his church, and to put food on the table he decided to give art lessons, sell greeting cards and develop film for the public. He put a sign on his front lawn advertising his services . . .

Without the metaphor this doesn't create much imagery. It is uninspired prose, and while we might find the character interesting, there's nothing here which will give us a word-picture of him.

But call the sign a monument, and suddenly we see that it marks the end of his life as a minister. The sign, which is his tombstone, makes that clear. It shows us instead of telling us, and the character takes on flesh and blood.

Metaphors must be approached cautiously because they are sensitive forms of expression, and overdone they can create havoc with surrounding prose. A testament to their consistent misuse is the filler that appears occasionally in *The New Yorker* . . . "Block That Metaphor," which details ludicrous attempts by writers who should know better. (Here's an example, taken from a well-known newspaper: "Australia recorded a slew of bankruptcies that cut a swath through the business dynamos who sprouted from the outback during the '80's." How do bankruptcies "cut a swath through" business dynamos?) If metaphor misuse finds its way into the pages of *The New Yorker,* we should understand that the matter is not insignificant, and that we skewer a metaphor at our peril.

That's not the way *I'd* want to appear in the magazine.

Fortunately, though, there are some things to guide us when we want to develop an effective metaphor. Columnist James Kilpatrick offers a couple of suggestions: "The first rule is to keep metaphors short . . . They are fragile affairs, incapable of bearing great weight . . ." He's right, generally, because we can overdo things so easily. It takes a master such as William Faulkner to run a metaphor through a chapter (as he did above—but, then, how many William Faulkners do we have?), so the thing to remember is . . . *short is beautiful!*

> *The day was a firestorm of disarray . . .*
>
> *Sometimes, when he smiled, his face would crack into an uneven grid of marbled whiteness . . .*

Keep metaphors as short as this and most problems will fall away.

James Kilpatrick goes on: "The second [rule] is to keep our metaphors internally consistent. If we fail to sustain a metaphor, we get into what has been termed a mixaphor . . ." We know it as a mixed metaphor, such as, "His eyes were red dots on the horizon" or "His clarinet shrilled the high notes, speaking to her with romantic fervor." In both cases the metaphor doesn't work because the image doesn't work. We don't have red dots on the horizon, red suns, perhaps, but even here the image seems tortured; if we want to be romantic, we don't "shrill" our message, we offer it gently. Mixed metaphors don't work, and we must be alert to their appearance, we must test them for their consistency and their relevance.

Similes should be weighed, too, and as with metaphors, they can become mixed and inappropriate:

> *The boys were as peppy and excited as a group of junkyard dogs . . .*
>
> *His voice carried like smoke from a chimney on a windy day . . .*

Neither one of these similes works because they don't call up the appropriate image: true, junkyard dogs can be active and raucous, but they can also be mean and snappy . . . is that what's meant here, that the boys were mean and snappy, too? We don't know, really, but unless the simile is more limited, and clearer, that's the sense we'll get.

And what does smoke look like when it rises from the chimney on a windy day? More often than not it disperses and disappears, or it flows away. In either case, it loses consistency and strength. Is that what's meant here—that the voice doesn't carry well? Here again, we don't know, but it's the sense we'll get, even if the writer is trying to tell us that the voice *does* carry well. At best the simile is confusing; at worst it's simply wrong.

"Keep your similes appropriate in subject," advises author Elyse Sommer, and it's something we all should remember. Don't allow the simile to stretch beyond the topic. Don't offer an image that doesn't square with the story. For example, if we are writing about the sea, a simile which compares and contrasts non-sea images will have a jolting effect which distorts the image we're trying to create; or if we're writing about a funeral, similes producing joyous, hand-clapping images will disturb the necessary mood. Think appropriateness, think consistency!

"Keep your similes appropriate in style," Elyse Sommer goes on. It seems that a simile which disrupts our style will simply not work well. For example, if we're writing a romance, and the style is dramatic and emotional, and we insert a simile which calls up disreputable, disagreeable images that repel our sensitivities, we've altered the style on the page.

> She emerged from the make-up department, her face smudged like a deep-shaft miner's with a day's residue of coal dust spotting his skin . . .

This type of image (unless the story actually is about the mining industry) is inappropriate for a romance. The blackened face of a miner at the end of his shift might tell us reams about the social conditions in the mines and

about the hard day's work that is required, but it's not
something that will add an emotional lift to a romance.
In style it's too matter-of-fact and unsavory image-
producing. Better we should write:

> She emerged from the make-up department, her
> face streaked with runaway mascara, her eyes glis-
> tening in a hundred star-points . . .

The difference is in the emotional reach. In the second
instance we have feelings portrayed with a semblance of
beauty; in the first we don't. In one case the style is
consistent, in the other it's not.

Now take a look at Joyce Carol Oates's book, *American
Appetites,* and watch how a simile can be extended down
the page, remaining consistent throughout. Here is a portrayal of Glynnis, Ian's wife, who dealt with people in an
interesting way:

> . . . and indeed, it sometimes seemed to Ian that his
> wife collected individuals with the avidity of an old-
> time biologist, hauling in and examining and classify-
> ing species. Ian, whose energy was drained by his
> work, whose imagination floundered when con-
> fronted by the mere prospect of cultivating a new
> friend, envied Glynnis both her will and her ability,
> was not, on the face of it, jealous; yet one day he
> would ask "where is Iris?" or "whatever became of—
> was her name Frances? I haven't seen her for months"
> and Glynnis would look at him blankly for a moment,
> before remembering. At such times Ian felt a slight
> chill, wondering if, at the start, he had not been one
> of Glynnis's specimens himself, which she had de-
> cided to keep . . .

On a quick reading this might seem like a metaphor, but
look carefully. Joyce Carol Oates is not saying that Glynnis
is an old-time biologist when it came to people, only that
she *acts* like one because of her penchant for dissecting

them; she is *like* an old-time biologist, and the author is able to carry the simile quite a distance because of her ability to compare Glynnis and the image of the old-time biologist. There are enough points of similarity for her to carry it into the short dialogue passage and retain the characteristics of the simile.

That is, she has taken the technique a step further than we might suppose. Instead of stopping after writing that Glynnis is *like* the old-time biologist, mentioning, of course, the hauling and examining and classifying, she then dramatizes the simile and gives it added dimension by including Ian's questions about the whereabouts of some of the specimen-people . . . and this has the effect of pumping up the drama level because we know that nothing serves drama so well as dialogue, even if it's short and the words of only one character. What Joyce Carol Oates had done is to provide a simile with a double charge: the basic image of the old-time biologist and the extended image of actual people (named, as well) who portray the image. Two whammies, two jolts, two chances for the reader to get the picture.

Can we do it? Of course. Remember first, that similes are "like" something else, and second, that the simile can create its own scene. So, we think of an object that could appear like something else:

> With each rush of wind, the tree-branch shadows were like long spidery fingers clutching the earth . . .

We have our simile. Now, let's dramatize it further:

> . . . "It's eerie out here," he said, "things keep moving around . . ."

We have dialogue added to the basic simile, and the image should be enhanced. Of course, we don't have to use dialogue to get this effect. We can do it with an appeal to the senses:

. . . His skin froze, he heard an eerie squeaking directly overhead, the blackness made it impossible to
see. *Did something touch him!* . . .

Or we can do it with melodrama:

. . . My God! The horror of his childhood dream,
eaten alive by carnivorous nature, ripped apart,
crunched between predatory teeth . . .

The basic simile, however, is the key to all this, and it
only works if it's appropriate in subject and style. Any
extension we make (dialogue, for instance) must be consistent with this as well.

We tend to think of similes in concrete terms: *her hair
was like . . . his book was like . . .* but there's nothing
that prevents us from using a simile with something intangible. It's the image we wish to develop, not the three-
dimensional object. *His views were like . . . her sympa-
thies were like . . .* these, too, can create images.

This is what Ward Just does in his novel, *The American
Ambassador,* set in Viet Nam in the 1970s. Gert, a young
German girl, is terrified of her father with whom she lives,
and she has seen him beat her mother numerous times.
Ward Just describes her reaction when they would come
upon one another in the house:

Often he would approach her, to say something or
to touch her hair or shoulder. She would hold herself
motionless, waiting for him to leave. Her mind would
commence to race, and the noise began. Her mind
was like a rushing stream, tumbling downhill over
rocks and boulders, eddying, bouncing, shifting direction. When next she looked up, he would be gone and
the words he had spoken vanished also, though if she
listened hard, she could discover them somewhere in
the room . . .

Here's a simile that isn't extended, yet it gives us a full

picture of a young woman in torment. "Her mind was like a rushing stream . . ." this is the simile, and the comparison is between something intangible—her mind, and something tangible—the rushing stream. The image is quite clear from all this, and we have no trouble understanding what she is going through and how she copes. The author doesn't need to extend the simile any further than he already has for the message to come through. He shows us Gert's torment.

Creating a simile out of the intangible requires only that we remember the basic rule about comparing and contrasting—*the fit must work*. An intangible with a tangible, providing it is appropriate, is fine.

> *His views were like his hands, rough and coarse and always dirty*
>
> *Her sympathies were like the oaks along her driveway, old and sturdy and unassuming . . .*

Imagery, remember imagery. Metaphors and similes are the tools to bring it all out.

So long as we understand it's the writer's *art* we're trying to develop.

6

Dialogue Sets the Pace

When I was thinking about being a writer, I sought out a family friend who happened to be an editor for a major publisher. I was relatively untrained, but I knew that technique played an important part in any written effort. Stories did not materialize from a puff of smoke; they were developed through hard work and application of learned skills—as well as a bedrock of creativity. I felt like a person sitting behind the controls of an exotic space craft, I knew the knobs and dials would allow me to fly, but I didn't know which ones to push and which ones to pull. I understood what it felt like to fly, but I wasn't sure how to get myself into the air.

"What's the most important thing a writer should know?" I asked.

"Everything's important." He smiled. "Nothing's unimportant."

"But there must be something that's more crucial than anything else. What do *you* look for in a manuscript, for instance?"

"I suppose it's dialogue," he said, "the way the writer handles dialogue."

I was surprised and said so.

"Think about it. Stories have characters and characters have to communicate. If the writer doesn't do that well, you've lost the spirit of the story. It becomes dull and boring."

He was right, of course, and he went on to tell me that a writer whose dialogue is wooden is a writer whose ability to imagine is severely restricted. "The writer has to *hear* those words, and that's only possible through an active imagination."

Good dialogue should accomplish one or both of the following:

- it must advance the story
- it must develop character

If it doesn't succeed with either of these, it doesn't belong in a story. As Anthony Trollope said, dialogue *must contribute to the telling of the story,* and the reason's apparent: dialogue which goes nowhere, which only decorates the page, blocks the story from going forward, and we know how long readers will stand for that!

But good dialogue, as opposed to static dialogue, serves a useful purpose because it carries dramatic impact, it *shows* rather than tells, and the reader can get immediately involved. Mystery writer Elmore Leonard has said that when he reads, he often skips down the page to the "interesting" parts, and invariably these are the dialogue passages. Anyone who has read Elmore Leonard can understand why he feels this way—his dialogue is as realistic and gripping as any fiction written today. His characters jump off the page, not because he has described them so well (though he does that with professional precision) but because of the way they communicate. Their words make them live in our minds.

Look at what dialogue can accomplish:

"I never begged," said Clara.

"He only asked for a sandwich," said Helen.

"I'm gonna give him a sandwich," Jack said.

"Jack don't want you to come back again," Francis said to Helen.

"I don't ever want to come back again," said Helen.

"He asked for a sandwich," Jack said. "I'll give him a sandwich."

"I knew you would," Francis told him.

"Damn right I'll give you a sandwich."

"Damn right," Francis said, "and I knew it."

"I don't want to be bothered," Clara said.

"Sharp cheese. You like sharp cheese?"

"My favorite," Francis said.

This is from *Ironweed,* William Kennedy's novel about the Depression and the derelicts that try to survive it in Albany, New York. Note there are four people in this scene: Clara, Jack, Helen and Francis, and Kennedy spins the dialogue among them. There are strong emotions depicted here, including hunger, anger, pride and kindness. Each dialogue passage tells us something about the speaker, and we sense the conflicts and the deep-seated desperation. There's plenty of drama here, and the dialogue displays it so we all can become involved.

The mistake people make with dialogue is to assume that what we say to one another in the course of the day or in the course of our lives can simply be transferred to the written page. If dialogue is conversation between two or more characters in a book, what is different about conversation between us and other people in real life? Conversation, in other words, and dialogue are the same thing.

WRONG!

What we say to one another and how those words are written are *not* the same thing. Think of conversations in the supermarket, on a street corner, over a cup of coffee, in the laundromat . . . how much of all that would trans-

fer to the written page so we could meet the two dialogue requirements:
- dialogue must advance the story
- dialogue must develop character

Not much of it, I would think. Readers read to be entertained, but when we converse, we may be seeking other things. Entertaining ourselves or entertaining others may or may not be a reason to have a conversation.

Yet, when we write, entertainment *is* our purpose.

Put it this way . . .

"Hello."

"Why, hello!"

"How are you?"

"I'm fine."

"That's good . . ."

Any drama here? Does the dialogue advance the story, give us insights into the characters? It's doubtful, yet this is conversation! This is the way we speak to one another. When it's translated to the written page, it slips into a dull recitation of unimportant mouthings. *Nothing is happening*.

So, written dialogue seeks to avoid this type of thing (as a general rule, "helloes" and "good-byes" are dialogue-*busters*, not dialogue-builders), and we start off a meeting between characters by launching right into the meat of their discussion. For example:

I spied Aunt Minnie hovering on the fringe of the group around grandfather, and I went over to her.

"You're looking well rested now," she said with a smile.

"The pain's almost gone," I said . . .

No helloes here, and when the two characters parted, there would be no good-byes either. Developing the drama is what we seek to do, and we can't get bogged down in simple conversation.

Take a look at the way Elizabeth Spencer handles it in

her novel, *Jack of Diamonds,* the story of Rosalind, her father and stepmother, Eva, who return to the father's lakeside cottage for the first time in three years. Rosalind's father has recently married Eva, shortly after the death of Rosalind's mother, and this is the first time Eva has seen the cottage. It's been a bittersweet return for Rosalind because of memories of her mother and her own early youth. On the last day she and her father take a boat and paddle out to an island in the lake.

"We aren't coming back," said Rosalind. "This is all."

"I saw you come in last night."

A bird flew up out of the trees.

"Did you tell Eva?"

"She was asleep. Why?"

"She'll think I sneaked off to see Fenwick. But I didn't. I went off myself . . . by myself."

He played with rocks seated, forearms resting on his knees, looking at the lake. "I won't tell."

"I wanted to find Mother."

"Did you?"

"In a way . . . I know she's here, all around here. Don't you?"

"I think she might be most everywhere . . ."

This is an emotional moment between father and daughter, and we learn some things about them. We see that the daughter has a more vivid recollection of the mother than does the father, and this colors her reaction to the return to the lakeside cottage. She yearns to get in touch with her dead mother, while the father has apparently come to terms with the memory. We also find out why Rosalind went out the night before, though at the time the author never did fill us in. Rosalind has simply left the house and wandered about for a while, but the author never let on that she was searching for her dead mother.

And we find out that Rosalind now believes this will be

the last time she and her father will be coming back to the house. (In fact, she's right because the father does put it on the market.) There's poignancy here and nostalgia, and all of it adds up to drama. Examine the dialogue passage carefully, and it's obvious that not one word is superfluous or doesn't contribute in some way to the story and its forward progress. The dialogue presents us with an emotional outpouring that we can feel, and if we can feel it, then we are involved in the story.

And if we are involved in the story, then the author has shown us and not told us!

Why does dialogue have the ability to create drama so easily? It personalizes everything by allowing us to *hear* what is being said as well as to read about it. We actually become part of the scene in this way, and the immediacy of the prose envelops us. Dialogue is not like narrative which reflects an expository mode and doesn't provide us the opportunity to "hear" the words as they are written because, of course, there's no live give-and-take.

But drama comes with the spoken word, and when we read it on the page, the word-sounds echo through our minds. It's never so clear as when we wish to portray tension and conflict.

"I don't want you to go near the lake."

"But Mom . . ."

"You don't know how to swim, Jimmy."

"It's not deep, I can stand . . ."

"No! It's too dangerous."

"You never let me . . ."

This is a familiar scene, but don't we hear the words again when we read the dialogue? We may recall them a bit differently, but the emotions are still the same, and so is the conflict, and the tension . . . a parent saying no, a youngster seeking adventure. If we had to do it in narrative, the effect wouldn't be the same, and the drama would lapse.

How about this?

"I've heard you know your way around a television studio," she said.

"I know which way the camera points," he said, smiling briefly.

"We're a tight little team here," she said, "the stars all shine alike."

"I get the feeling you're telling me something . . ."

A different kind of tension, but dramatic, nevertheless. Once more we should be able to *hear* the words, as well as read them, and we should be able to imagine the scene and the two people confronting one another. We should have a word-picture in our minds.

Now take a look at this selection from Scott Turow's *The Burden of Proof* which is the story of attorney Sandy Stern whose wife, Clara, commits suicide in the opening pages of the book. Stern is haunted by why his wife would do such a thing, and he discovers that his next door neighbor, Nate Cawley, a doctor, had been treating her for genital herpes, and he assumes it was Cawley who infected her. He threatens to sue him for contributing to her death on the grounds that Clara took her life because she could no longer face the ignominy of her disease. But he then finds out that Nate Cawley was only treating her for the symptoms of the disease, that someone else had infected her. So, they meet at Sandy Stern's house and Stern tells Cawley he will not be sued.

The two men looked at each other. Nate, chilled by the house's air conditioning, rubbed his arms.

"She spoke to you of this impulse, I take it?" asked Stern. "Ending her life?"

"She did," said Nate. "She had a way of talking about it." Nate posed, studying the air so he could recall. "She said she wanted to put out the noise. Something like that. You know, she didn't always go on that way, but over seven years when things got bad, I'd hear it once in a while. And I can't pretend I didn't take her seriously."

Nothing, for an instant: no sound, no time. *"Seven years,"* the man had said. Looking down, Stern realized he'd taken a chair.

"Seven years, Nate?"

"God—I'd assumed—" Nate stopped. "Well how would you know?" he asked himself. "Sandy this wasn't a new condition. It was a recurrence?"

This is obviously an emotional scene, made more dramatic by the dialogue which can capture the feelings of the participants instantly. Look at what we have . . . Nate's relief at not being sued—Sandy's shock and disbelief that his late wife had herpes for seven years—Nate's description of Clara's discussion about taking her own life—and Clara's reaction to having the disease and the image she calls up ("putting out the noise") in order to deal with it. This is heavy stuff, and I suppose we could describe all of it by means of narrative so the reader will get the same information, but it certainly won't be with the same amount of drama. See how a bit of it reads in narrative:

. . . Nate Cawley told Sandy Stern that Clara had a way of talking about her impending suicide. She told him that she wanted to put out the noise, or something like that, and over the seven years he treated her he'd hear her say it once in a while . . .

Isn't the dialogue more effective? There's immediacy and reader involvement, whereas in the narrative it's more like a photograph. We look and appreciate, perhaps, but we don't feel a part of it. When Sandy exclaims, "Seven years, Nate?" we know his voice is tight, his eyes are enlarged, perhaps his chin is set and his mind is spinning. Since we can *hear* his words, we get a fix on what he sounds like, and if the image blossoms a bit more, we'll *see* him in the chair.

Narrative can't perform these little miracles, at least not without some additional help (see Chapter Eleven for what narrative *can* do). But dialogue has the power to put us into the middle of the scene, to make us characters in the on-going story, to involve us in the tensions and the conflicts wherever they might be. Dialogue *is* drama . . .

And drama *shows,* it never tells.

7

Now Comes Melodrama

Here's a scene we've witnessed:

It's Wednesday night in the middle of the school term and sixteen year old daughter should have been home two hours ago. Mother and Dad sit in the den pretending to stare at television. Mother sighs audibly and receives a reassuring smile from Dad.

The front door opens. "Hi! I'm home."

Mother springs to her feet, storms into the hall.

"Where have you *been*? My God, we were getting frantic!"

"Oh Mother! Jeff's car had a flat."

"Why didn't you phone?" Dad says.

"From the lake? Get real. Everything's closed."

"You could have been killed!" says Mother.

"I'm sixteen years old!"

"You're still a baby!"

"God, you're melodramatic," says daughter, running upstairs . . .

Through recent decades, melodramic expression has developed the tarnish of overwriting and overeffect. It's storytelling over the edge of believability, and its literary value is often questioned. To be accused of writing melo-dramatically is like being chastened for slurping our soup or chewing with our mouths open.

It's simply not done, and anyone in good literary company would know better.

So say the purists.

Well, I've never been a purist, either at the dinner table or at my writer's desk, though I can be table-mannered, if I must. But the writing desk has its own rules, and suffering purists gladly is not one of them—at least at *my* writing desk.

If melodrama can add pizzazz to a piece of writing, why shouldn't it be allowed to sparkle? If melodrama can reach out and hug the reader, why keep it straitjacketed?

Ah, I know what people will say . . . melodrama is un-real and forced, it reeks of farce and silly posturing. It is heavy-handed.

All true, I suppose, if we freeze-frame our consideration to silent movie days when the evil landlord (with the ubiquitous thin moustache, of course) demands the over-due rent from the honey-dipped, sweet-eyed maiden while the piano-player records every emotional nuance with crashing certitude.

But melodrama has become much more than this (as the scene with the sixteen-year-old daughter attests), and while its past is—ah, checkered—melodrama's present is more robust. It has become a writer's tool, and an effec-tive one at that, for blocking the urge to tell all.

Melodrama, properly used, is one of the show-all good guys. It is exaggeration, to be sure, overdramatization, sensationalism, and many times it is inappropriate (as when the scene has no place for extravagant emotion). But there are times when melodramatic writing can truly hit the mark, when its dramatic effect can carry an entire scene—or even an entire book.

In *The Vampire Lestat*, Ann Rice has fashioned a charac-ter beyond simple exaggeration—a vampire. This is someone of mythic proportion, unreal in our three-dimensional world but quite real in the fields of our fantasy. This is the evil landlord in drag, modernized and fleshed out. Here's the way she has her vampire describe itself after the third night of its return to our earth:

> I wore gorgeous black leather clothes that I'd taken from my victims, and I had a little Sony Walkman stereo in my pocket that fed Bach's Art of the Fugue through tiny earphones right into my head as I blazed along.
>
> I was the vampire Lestat again. I was back in action. New Orleans was once again my hunting ground.
>
> As for my strength, well, it was three times what it had been. I could leap from the street to the top of a four-story building, I could pull iron gratings off windows. I could bend a copper penny double. I could hear human voices and thoughts, when I wanted to, for blocks around . . .

Here is exaggeration on a grand scale, a vampire living among us with interests as human as good classical music and as inhuman as hunting down victims to feast on their blood. The melodramatic effect in all this comes in two ways: first, there is the contrast between the human and the inhuman with both urges residing in the same character—thus, the vampire catches our interest and imagination, even though, we know, we *really* know such a character does not exist—except in our imagination which records all the exaggerations of the prose. Second, it is these exaggerations—the overwhelming physical and mental strengths—that provide a jump-start to the action because we can sense what their effects will be on anything that might happen. A vampire let loose among the humans in New Orleans is little different from the object of a well-worn aphorism:

Q: What do you do with a 600-pound gorilla?

A: Anything he wants to do.

And that's what creates the drama here. A character beyond human control whose effect on the story may be overwhelming. It's the same idea, really, as the evil landlord and his effect on the innocent maiden . . . except, of course, that the landlord is human. (But, then, Ann Rice portrays her vampire as human, too—at least in many respects.) The landlord is exaggerated evil and so is the vampire. Melodrama on a contemporary scale.

Why does melodrama work here? It forces us to exercise our imaginations simply to picture the characters and the events that will occur; there's no way we can avoid it. By its nature melodrama forces the imagination to work because we can't grasp characters and action any other way. Melodrama *shows*.

Any determined writer can put together melodramatic effects, though we must remember that the scene should lend itself to high emotion and/or outsized characters. Sedate circumstances or characterizations which rely on subtlety will not work well. For melodrama to be effective it must burst upon the reader and inundate him or her with effects and consequences. It must explode!

- A man reacts to his wife's affair and climbs on a window ledge, threatening to jump.
- A woman wails and tears her clothing because a pet dog has been struck by a car.
- A man turns into a lion by night and hunts fresh human meat.

Exaggeration, to be sure, but our imaginations haven't shut down, not when they have to face *these* situations.

Emotion plays an important part in melodrama. To a large extent it is *the* driving force. Think back to that evil landlord once more, ask ourselves what is it about that scene which makes it so outsized, and the answer is the presence of fear and greed—two utterly basic emotions and characteristics. The more we emphasize them by the way the characters speak or in what they say or do, the more outsized everything becomes, until the level of exaggeration is so high it becomes melodrama.

But melodrama isn't limited to exaggerated fear and greed. Everything's fair game—anger, sadness, pomposity, ineffectiveness. In fact, one of the most fertile subjects is the opposite of fear and greed.

Romance.

Love, attraction, beauty, joy. The happy emotions. Here, just as with the sinister, frightening aspects of fear and greed, there is room for melodrama. Romance, in fact, is a natural for melodrama because it is saturated with emotion, and where the emotional cue takes hold, emotional fill-up will happen. A romance can't sputter along on one emotional cylinder, it must carry through to all the characters who will be affected in the story. Look at Shakespeare's *Romeo and Juliet*, for instance. There's love between the two young people . . . and hate between the two families. Emotions in both circumstances are so outsized that they could rise to melodrama. The level of hate is sufficient to justify murder and assassination, while the level of love is sufficient to cause the lovers to die. These are pretty strong consequences to develop from bare emotions, yet they seem justifiable enough under the circumstances.

The reason?

The story is sufficiently developed so the reader never doubts that these things could happen, that murder and suicide, all in the name of family affairs, could take place, *within the circumstances of the story*. The same thing occurs with *The Vampire Lestat*. We'd have trouble believing a vampire could be among us except for the fact the vampire is fleshed out to such an extent that it acquires human dimension.

And then we believe.

Romance works the same way, only here we can zero in on the emotional content completely. And it doesn't matter whether we pile too much emotion on, either. Author David Madden says, "The romantic's over-reaching often ends in melodramatic effect, but that is sometimes what we go to the romantic for. The classic writer strains to avoid the false; the romantic is willing to risk seeming false by classical standards to achieve his own, new effects."

The "new effects" Madden refers to are the waves of emotion that course through the pages, catching the reader up in a bath of feeling. The heavier the emotions, the greater the potential impact, and the more opportunity there will be for reader identification. Make no mistake about it—readers like to grasp emotional content, they enjoy deep feelings and high joy, even where such emotions might seem inappropriate. Readers want to be *entertained*, and sometimes reality only gets in the way.

Melodrama carries with it a note of falsity, to be sure, but at the same time it forces us to think emotional content, and this is where the dramatic effects in any piece of writing usually are. When we develop a melodramatic scene or circumstance, we cannot fall back on telling. It simply won't work. Melodrama means showing. Consider these choices:

> Her face was pinched with anger, and her voice grew shrill. She was absolutely furious to discover her favorite bowl of strawberries had been eaten . . .

—

> "There's a thief in this house!" she shouted. "I hate food-stealing. Call the police!"
>
> "Mother, please . . ."
>
> "I will not abide someone eating my strawberries," she said. "Jail's too good for them."

In the first example we have no melodrama, only a description of someone's anger, and the result is "telling." But in the second choice we use dialogue and we can portray that anger, and its outsized form becomes melodrama. This is "showing."

Since romantic writing is intimately tied with emotion, it becomes a natural for melodramatic effect. Which of us hasn't resorted to emotional hyperbole during the course of a romantic incident? Which of us hasn't projected outsized emotions during a romantic interlude? It's natural to be swept away, and the romance writer understands what needs to be done.

Take this selection from Barbara Taylor Bradford, whose many novels maintain a staunch romantic flavor. In *The Women In His Life* she tells the story of Maximillian West, a hugely successful businessman, and she follows him from his early twenties to late middle age. One day, in his youth, he is in a book shop and his eyes meet those of a beautiful woman, Anastasia, but before he can speak to her she disappears. He fears he will never see her again, but the next evening at a supper dance he sees her speaking to his friend, Stubby, across the room and he walks right over.

"I thought I'd lost you," Maxim said, after Stubby left. He was staring at her, continuing to hold her hand. "Actually, I thought I'd never find you again."

"I knew we'd meet," she responded with the same kind of unself-conscious honesty.

"You did?" he sounded surprised.

"Oh yes, I was certain."

"Why? I mean, what made you so sure?"

"It's destiny."

He paused, peered at her. "Are you saying that I am your destiny, Anastasia?"

"Yes. And I am yours."

"I hope to God you are."

How realistic is it to expect people who have never met one another to speak this way? Yet in a romantic setting does it seem out of place? These are extravagant emotions and words, melodramatic because they burst beyond what we'd normally expect between a man and a woman on first meeting. But they feed our pleasure, too, because the emotional content of the scene is so strong and *we can imagine what is being said and how it is being said*. We identify with the scene and the characters in spite of its exaggerated sense.

Why? Because we know we're being entertained, and we're willing to forgive most anything in the name of entertainment. Would two people *really* say these things to one another on first meeting? Probably not, but can we *imagine* people saying these things? Of course.

That's showing, not telling.

Many of today's melodramatic effects have their roots in the dime novels of the nineteenth century where realism was subordinated to entertainment on almost every page. Bigger-than-life characters facing overwhelming dangers, unimagined in most of the civilized world at that time, entertained a rousing audience for decades. No one thought of these writings as mirrors of reality, yet each reader could imagine the adventures and the dangers and the escapes that played out on the pages. Here was showing to its ultimate level.

Now, many decades and several generations later, the concept of melodrama has broadened to involve almost any writing style. As well as in romance writing, we can find melodrama in humor (where the idea of exaggeration is crucial for comic effect), in satire, in mystery-suspense. We can even find it in what has come to be called "social criticism," to point out flaws or inequities in the way some people live. This isn't satire (though it could be, of course), but it overdramatizes in order to help the reader to understand.

Take a look at Erskine Caldwell's *Tobacco Road*, a novel set in the 1930s about poor whites in North Carolina and their unending struggle to live and survive. The book achieved notoriety in two ways: it was banned from some schools and libraries because of certain erotic scenes and coarse language, and it was criticized because it skewered the established social order where the landholding, business-owning elite did little but exploit their legions of workers. The latter was the social criticism that could lend itself to melodrama. See how the author describes life on and off the farm:

> "I reckon old Jeeter had the best thing happen to him," Lou said. "He was killing himself all the time about the raising of a crop. That was all he wanted in this life—growing cotton was better than anything else to him. There ain't many more like him left, I reckon. Most of the people now don't care about nothing except getting a job in a cotton mill somewhere. But can't all of them work in the mills, and they'll have to stay here like Jeeter until they get taken away too. There ain't no sense in them raising crops. They can't make no money at it, not even a living . . ."

Such a dismal picture the author paints! Those that want to farm won't be able to earn a living, and those that go to work in the cotton mills will have to endure long hours and small pay and a struggle for respectability. The cotton mills seem preferable, if only because the work and pay are more reliable, but what happens if a man wants to work for himself, if he wants to farm some land?

He'll starve. Jeeter was "killing himself all the time about the raising of a crop" . . . Most people, like Jeeter, will be "taken away too" . . .

This is melodrama because it offers the most disagreeable consequences to the basic human desire to work independently. Caldwell says it was impossible, but he doesn't *tell* us it was impossible . . . he shows us by having one character—through dialogue—describe Jeeter to another and by contrasting what Jeeter went through with what others will have to face. The key is to present the worst-case result and then to dramatize it. Suppose, for example, we wanted to create stories of social criticism, using melodramatic effect. We might zero in this way:

    young-executive materialism: greedy, acquisitive people who brag of accomplishments and degrade others.

    anti-abortion: it has become the law of the land, there are "abortion" police and women must submit to periodic "fertility" tests; a violation is considered pre-meditated murder.

These stories would take social criticism to the outer limits in order to make a point. They could rely on melodrama because the point can be made so much easier, and that's the purpose of social criticism—getting the reader to understand an imbalance in the social order.

"My God! Is it really *that* bad!"

Melodrama saves the day.

8

Anecdotes Paint the Picture

Through the ages, legions of children have urged:
    "Tell me a story"...
Teachers and parents have decided:
    "It's story time"...
Yarn spinners have announced:
    "I know a story"...
The idea of the *story* as an event which arrests attention and creates excitement is a mark of human heritage and stretches to the beginnings of recorded time. In the third verse of Genesis, for example, after the creation of the world and the creation of man and woman, comes the story of the serpent in the Garden of Eden. "Is it true that God has forbidden you to east from any tree in the garden?" the serpent asks Eve. She answers:

    "We may eat the fruit of any tree in the garden, except for the tree in the middle of the garden; God has forbidden us either to eat or to touch the fruit of that; if we do, we shall die."

The serpent convinces her that will not happen, and so she eats the fruit and gives some to her husband, Adam. The third verse goes on:

Then the eyes of both of them were opened and they discovered that they were naked; so they stitched fig-leaves together and made themselves loincloths.

The story continues with the appearance of God who delivers a curse that will burden all of them and their descendants forever.

The *story* as an art form is useful and popular because it stands as a mirror for our own lives. "Tell me a story," the child asks, and soon the child enters that make-believe world and becomes part of the story. "I know a story," a writer might say, and the characters begin to blossom in the writer's mind and some connection with what the writer knows or has experienced will develop. Readers will identify or become involved in the story because they recognize parts of themselves or someone they are familiar with. The *story* offers the opportunity to gaze at the mirror and measure ourselves.

And the *story* is a way of showing us to the world. It is drama and excitement and involvement. We are not being held at arm's length, nor are we having things explained, as if at a lecture. We are the story.

Writer's understand that the story—in enlarged or sliced-off form—goes by the name of anecdote which is a tale buried within the text of a larger and longer narrative. All of us communicate in anecdotes . . . "You hear what Harry did yesterday?". . ."Friends, speaking here today reminds me of the time I first saw this building". . ."Your Honor, I'd like to ask this witness what she saw when she looked out her window that night". . . .

Anecdotes are happenings that might be as small as a few words or as lengthy as several pages, but they are crucial to developing drama and creating a word-picture. Every joke-teller is relating an anecdote, for example, even though it may be clear fantasy or nonsense. "You ever hear the one about . . . ?" and we are launched into an anecdote. Most song lyrics, if they are comprehensible, are anecdotal because they describe a happening, a series of events. Every confessional experience, religiously based or not, is anecdotal because we are relating something said or done against a background of facts and circumstances; we are offering a *story*.

It's no different on the written page. If we wish to dramatize our prose, an anecdote or two will work well. From their earliest days in journalism school or in a newsroom, most journalists understand that the way to gain a reader's attention is by means of an anecdote, particularly as the "lead." It is a major source of story openings:

> On the morning of his twenty-sixth birthday, Bob Wilson had no clue that by nightfall, his world would be turned upside down. Recently married, he had quietly given up most habits of his bachelor life, except for two overweening pleasures—horses and the dollar-a-week lottery ticket he bought from Hucky Hun, the Korean dwarf who operated a coffee truck at the train station . . .

Here is a story in the making, and by the time we have read this far we should be hooked. The fact that the story might be about lottery winners (or losers) and that it might examine what motivates people to take the gamble is barely touched in this opening. We have a *story*, and now readers want to know what's going to happen to Bob Wilson. In another paragraph or two we'll switch to the real meat of the piece—the examination of the lottery motive— but the Bob Wilson vignette will stay with the reader as an example of what we're about to explore. And because Bob Wilson is a person and his story is a personal revelation, the reader will be drawn in. We've made it possible for the reader to feel involved and to identify—in this instance with Bob Wilson. We haven't started the piece with a lecture or an explanation about lotteries or about why people buy lottery tickets. We started with a *story*, and that has given the reader a base with which to consider the less dramatic portions to follow.

An anecdote need not come at the opening, of course, and non-fiction writers readily use it elsewhere (fiction writers do, as well). But the purpose of the anecdote doesn't change (whether nonfiction or fiction); it's a way of dramatizing something to make it more understandable and more significant. If we take the Bob Wilson story and develop it, we might find ourselves continuing the anecdote at a mid point in the piece, that is, after we've already done some exposition and narrative. Then a shift back to Bob Wilson and how his day will turn upside down should keep the reader intrigued—and probably guessing.

Fiction writers use anecdotes all the time, and for the same reasons: they will dramatize, they will *show*, they will develop reader involvement. The difference is that the anecdote in fiction must develop from the text of the story; the story, itself, proceeds along, and then the anecdote must be woven into the prose—a story inside a story. For example:

> . . . the day had been hot and muggy, and he had tried not to stir from his air-conditioned bed-sitter. His waiting like this reminded him of the blistery July in Paris when his contact from Algiers had been more than three days overdue. Finally, he had called the safe number, and a female voice had asked him . . .

We can make the anecdote as long or as short as we wish, but we must not forget that it has to have a purpose; it must advance the story, somehow, either by delineating character a bit or by advancing the plot. In the example, the story about the Algiers connection must show us something of the character's past so we can understand him more easily now, or it must present an event which will have a bearing on the plot at some later time. Once we're clear on the purpose, the anecdote becomes important.

A common approach is to add an anecdote in the middle of a narrative passage. It can serve two uses: it will break up the unrelieved narrative (and hence keep the reader's attention through a modified change of pace) and it will add drama, giving the reader a chance to enjoy a *story*. In the hands of an accomplished novelist it works well. See how George Higgins handles it in *Kennedy for the Defense*, his story of Jerry Kennedy, a criminal defense lawyer in Boston, who is an expert on his own city. Higgins takes three pages to narrate the route from the Parker House Hotel to Kennedy's office at 80 Boylston Street, mentioning landmarks, streets, corners and buildings. Finally, in the office waiting room he describes the chairs and mentions they came from a Dr. Edward Carey, one of Kennedy's clients, who was getting a divorce and needed money.

> Dr. Carey wrote a lot of prescriptions. Many of them, if not close to all of them, were for people whom he had not diagnosed, or, indeed, even examined. He had never laid eyes on them in his life. He seldom knew their names. The names he wrote on the prescriptions were real, but they were names that happened to be listed in the South Suburban phone book. The people who got the prescriptions filled were not the same . . .

Higgins continues the saga of Dr. Carey for another half page, describing how Dr. Carey gets caught and goes to prison and must now sell everything to pay attorney fees, as well as a fine . . . and that's how Jerry Kennedy was able to get his office furniture.

Here, now, is an anecdote in the midst of a lengthy narrative about the city of Boston and the furnishings in attorney Kennedy's office. The story of Dr. Carey shows us two things: Jerry Kennedy's opportunistic side where he was able to get office furniture from what modestly could be called a "motivated seller," and the fact that Jerry Kennedy is well aware of the seamier side of things in the Boston legal world. The anecdote, itself, does not advance the plot (once we've finished with the story of Dr. Carey, he doesn't appear again, nor does any further reference to the office furniture), but it does show us some facets of Jerry Kennedy's personality. Higgins might have told us Kennedy was opportunistic or that the office furniture came from an ex-client who had to go to jail and left it at that. Instead, he chose to provide an anecdote about Dr. Carey which has the effect of putting some flesh on Jerry Kennedy so the reader can imagine him more fully, and it also breaks up the lengthy three-page narrative about the tour from the Parker House to Kennedy's office. The reader's sense of involvement has to profit from all of this, and the dramatic impact of the anecdote has to make the writing more enjoyable.

There's nothing that says dialogue can't be included in an anecdote; in fact it will add to the overall dramatic impact. We know from Chapter Six that use of dialogue is a way of gaining immediacy for the reader and establishing story identity, so if it can be added within the anecdote, its effect will be to enhance the sense of *story*. Take the example of the joke teller: we've all been exposed to the situation where conversation trips along on a level plain, and someone says, "That reminds me of a joke . . ." The joke teller begins, and if he or she is any good, the joke will include lines such as:

"He said . . ."
"So she said . . ."
"And then he said . . ."

A back-and-forth rendering of dialogue to give the joke authenticity and to maintain a certain sense of drama. If the joke teller is exceedingly good, there may even be passable mimicry. But the point is that the joke, which is really nothing but an anecdote, breaks the conversation level, establishes a change of pace and offers a story.

Writers do the same thing. If we are in the midst of narrative and want to break it up with an anecdote, we don't have to keep the anecdote in narrative form. We can use dialogue in the anecdote, and it's perfectly natural, a "he said," "she said" excursion:

> . . . walking up Terrill's Hill. He knew he'd be late, but nobody really cared. One more foster home was all it was. He wished he could still be with the Blakelys. He remembered Mom B. the first day, "Our home is your home," she had said, and he had stammered something about a baseball mitt outside the door. "Would you like to use it?" she had asked . . .

We approach the anecdote the same way we approach the overall story, and what's appropriate for the story is certainly appropriate for an anecdote. Dialogue, narrative, or any point in between, we use whatever technique will give the anecdote a worthwhile purpose. Take a look at the way Ann Beattie handles something that isn't quite dialogue and isn't quite narrative, yet offers a clear and convincing dramatic impact. In her novel, *Chilly Scenes of Winter*, she shows us Charles, a young man in his twenties and unmarried, now back living in the house where he grew up. He contemplates his old room and wants to change it around:

> Moving the bed is a bigger problem. He pushes hard, bunching the rug underneath the bed. He lifts the bottom of the bed and pushes the rug with his foot. He hopes that he does not get a hernia. There was a boy in the sixth grade who had a hernia that had to be operated on. The class sent him a card. Nobody knew what message to write, so almost everybody

wrote: "I am sorry you have a hernia. See you soon." Some people asked how the food was. One girl refused to sign the card. She told the teacher that her mother would write a note saying she didn't have to. The teacher said it wasn't necessary.

He gave the bed a final shove . . .

The anecdote about the card serves the purpose of breaking up Charles's private examination of his room and giving further insight to Charles's character and background. It provides a story which can spur our imaginations perhaps to the point where we picture the young girl who has refused to sign the card. We can imagine the school scene where the classmates circulate the card, and each one, in turn, contemplates whether to sign it and what to write. It's a common enough schoolroom scene; many of us, if we think back, can remember something like it during our own young lives, yet here it serves as an anecdote. And because it is something many of us have experienced, we can certainly relate to it.

But note this, too: the author *quotes* the most common comment; it isn't dialogue exactly, yet it is more than simple narrative. The quote marks make the difference, and once we see those our interest-antennae rise. She could have written:

. . . almost everybody wrote that they were sorry he had a hernia and that they'd see him soon . . .

But she didn't. She made the comment into a quote, and by doing this she added drama to her anecdote. It made it more identifiable and involving for the reader, and *showed* how the children—and Charles—were feeling.

It makes the anecdote even more of a story.

But there are all kinds of stories, and we shouldn't expect anecdotes to follow any special pattern (except that they should show and dramatize and have purpose). We've seen they can be parables (from The Bible) as well

as character builders and plot movers, but they might also
develop settings, offer a change in point of view, create a
philosophic underpinning. As stories, anecdotes are a way
for the writer to get his or her point across to the reader
without resorting to lengthy explanation, and there's no
limit on the different techniques that might be used: fantasy or reality, historical or futuristic, interior monologue
or exterior dialogue . . . it doesn't matter *so long as the
anecdote is a story and has purpose.*

Mark Twain was masterful at using anecdotes, and he
wasn't bound by the usual approach: "That reminds me of
a story . . ." For him anecdotes could serve several purposes, such as moving a plot as well as offering a philosophic point of view. In *The Adventures of Huckleberry
Finn*, for example, he also utilizes foreshadowing. Huck
and Jim are paddling their way on the Mississippi near
Cairo, Illinois, with Huck in a canoe and Jim on the raft.
They get separated in the current and dense fog, and after
some anxious hours finally find one another. Jim confesses
he went to sleep and had a dream about some of the river
sights he had passed. Huck narrates the story:

> Then he said he must start in and 'terpret it, because
> it was sent as a warning. He said the first towhead
> stood for a man that would try to do us some good,
> but the current was another man that would get us
> away from him. The whoops was warnings that
> would come to us every now and then, and if we
> didn't try hard to make out to understand them
> they'd just take us into bad luck, 'stead of keeping us
> out of it. The lot of towheads was troubles we was
> going to get into with quarrelsome people and all
> kinds of mean folks, but if we minded our business
> and didn't talk back and aggravate them, we would
> pull through . . .

This dream interpretation is an anecdote within the saga of Huck and Jim riding the Mississippi, and while it isn't the usual kind of *story*, it does offer foreshadowing and tension build-up. What Jim prophesies will come true, and the reader is now touched with curiosity about it. The fact that Jim mentions some unpleasant future experiences for them both will keep the reader's attention and provide an additional level of interest in the overall story. But it is the use of the technique of foreshadowing that is masterful here; customarily, we think of anecdotes as straightforward stories, yet there is nothing that prevents their being used to serve other purposes, and so long as we show something happening, we have the makings of a story, even if it is more parable than vividly plotted.

And that's what happens here. Jim's dream interpretation suggests what is going to happen, instead of what is happening at that moment, and this, really, is the way an anecdote works—it changes the focus of the story, if only momentarily. Up to Jim's dream interpretation the story described the journey down the Mississippi, but suddenly the focus changes—now we have fantasy and foreshadowing, yet we still have a story: Jim's dream interpretation. It's got a plot and it has characters.

And it offers a moral lesson: try hard to understand those things which could bring you into bad luck . . . mind your business, don't talk back, don't aggravate quarrelsome people. It's the parable of the outsider, of course, the one who seeks peace and tranquility in what could easily be a mean, mean world.

And can any of us deny our mind's image of Jim earnestly talking to Huck and 'terpreting his dream?

That's showing, folks.

9

Incidents = Movement

Remember the nineteen sixties and the so-called "happenings?" There were "sit-ins" and "love-ins" and "teach-ins" and finally, as a general comment on the social nature of the phenomenon, there was the "be-in" which meant that someone had to *be somewhere*. No other purpose was needed.

"Be-ins" occurred in department store rotundas or the bleachers at a major league ball game or on a crowded street corner. "Let's have a 'be-in'," someone would suggest, and in that souped-up atmosphere of arrogant certainty and establishment-baiting, crowds would stream to the spot, understanding vaguely that simple presence guaranteed a form of success.

"It's a 'be-in'!" shouts would ring out. "We're here!"

A "happening" it was called.

Sometimes it was a non-happening, purposeless drifting that meant little and dissolved to nothingness. But even here the scene was not blank. People came, and that meant there was *potential*, a possibility of something taking place. Human dynamics abhor a vacuum, so a non-happening couldn't remain that way for long, and soon there would be . . . something, an event, movement, a development!

The idea of the "happening" is the real-life counterpart of the writer's need to produce "incident" in fiction or nonfiction. A happening is an incident and an incident is a happening; it is action in real life and a storytelling tool on the written page. It creates interest no matter its venue.

Think, again, of those 1960s "be-ins." If there was a purpose or a theme to follow, the happening brought an abrupt change to the atmosphere where it took place. A "love-in," for example, meant swarms of young people congregating for purposes of love-making in a public park or on a beach or in an empty house, and no one— participant or spectator—could remain unaffected by what went on. Something was definitely happening.

Now translate this to the written page and make it a story. Let's write about a "love-in," only let's start the story a few moments or a few hours before the love-in occurs. We have characters converging on the scene of the event, some who will participate, some who won't, and some who aren't aware it will take place. If the setting is to be a public park, the atmosphere among those unaware of the coming love-in might be picnic-like with relaxed, family-oriented dialogue. There's a somnolence to the story at this point, and perhaps the writer can take the time to examine one or more of the characters in depth.

Then, the vanguard of the "love-in" arrives, and suddenly the story atmosphere changes. At first there's mild curiosity on the part of the innocent picnickers because the young people have a certain unrestrained charm, but the picnickers soon realize what is really going to happen, and their attitude changes to embarrassment, followed by anger and disgust. They decide to leave, but not before making some contact with the young people, and their feelings are made known. At this point, story-tension is achieved, and I leave the possibilities for plot development to any imaginative writer.

But the point is that the "love-in" is an incident in the overall story, and it affects the atmosphere. See what it accomplishes:

- it changes the pace
- it heightens the tension
- it provides a counterpoint to the picnickers' values
- it introduces new characters

All of these mean that there has been a "happening," an event which has triggered movement in the plot. Things in the story are no longer the way they were. The incident also pushes the reader's imagination because it is an abrupt change in the storyline, and there must be some attempt to visualize the scene in order to taste the flavor of the action. In other words the incident—any incident—is a form of "showing" because it calls upon the reader to imagine an event or a circumstance different from what has gone on before.

Suppose there's a quiet dinner party in progress, and a baby cries from one of the bedrooms. Is this an incident?

Suppose there's a routine medical examination, and the possibility of contamination by cholera is discovered. Is this an incident?

Suppose the stock market collapses, and a bank holiday is declared? Is this an incident?

The answer is yes to all three because something new and different has been added to the story. An incident is exactly that—something new and different. Whether it's a baby's cry or cholera infection or a bank holiday, something is happening, and this creates the opportunity for a dramatic portrayal. Note that each of these vignettes contains the same characteristics as the "love-in": they develop tension, change of pace, counterpoint and new characterizations. They create a new and different scene, and the storyline must include them.

Look to the theatre for a worthwhile comparison. The playwright knows that there had better be action and movement on the stage if the audience isn't going to fall asleep; characters had better keep in motion, and events had better continue to transpire. How's it done? Unless it's a soliloquy, there's a steady stream of "stage business" where characters stand up or sit down, move, depart or enter stage left or stage right, pick something up or set it down, so the audience's attention remains transfixed. There are noises, voices off stage and events which occur even though the audience never sees them, and the effect is to move the story along by changing pace and developing tension.

Each time an unseen voice sounds, we have an incident.

Each time one character has a confrontation on stage with another character, we have an incident.

Each time thunder and lightning flash on stage (or off stage), we have an incident.

Something new and different. A change of pace. Tension.

In the hands of an accomplished writer, incident can become the focal point of a story. In John Sayles's short story, "At the Anarchist's Convention," a group of elderly ex-radicals meet for a reunion at a mid-town New York hotel. They reminisce about their early struggles, their lost comrades and enemies, the jail sentences many of them served, the demonstrations they organized and carried out, the internal feuding that went on, the exciting times when they banded against any form of authority. Many of them are quite infirm now, and there's quavering nostalgia in the way they glance back at their lives. Then, near the end of the story comes the key incident:

And then the hotel manager walks in. Brown blazer,

twenty dollar haircut and a smile from here to Salt
Lake City. A huddle at the platform. Baker and Mr.
Manager bowing and scraping at each other, Bud
Odum looking grim, Weiss turning colors. Sophie and
I go up, followed by half the congregation. Nobody
trusts to hear it secondhand. I can sense the sweat
breaking under that blazer when he sees us coming,
toothless, gnarled, suspicious by habit. Ringing
around him, the Anarchist's Convention.

"A terrible mistake," he says

"All my fault," he says

"I'm awfully sorry," he says, "but you'll have to
move". . .

He tells the old anarchists that the Rotary Club from
Sioux Falls had already booked the room when he had
agreed to let them have the space. They were outside the
room "full of gin and boosterism" and demanding what
they had reserved.

The old anarchists refuse to leave, and suddenly it's like
one of those old battles, fighting the forces of the estab-
lishment. They link arms, sing the old political songs and
dare the manager to remove them. Smiles come to their
faces, blood courses through their bodies, they are reliv-
ing the most exciting times of their lives. . . .

And the aging pains and the uncertain memories are no
longer in evidence.

This story is wonderfully humorous and poignant at the
same time, and the reader can't help but visualize a group
of seventy-year-olds (or older) confronting the slick hotel
manager with their old street tactics, linking arms and
refusing to budge. At a time when we tend to think of
elderly people seeking tranquility and comfort here is a
group looking to do exactly the opposite.

The key in the story, however, is the incident when the
hotel manager comes in to remove them. Up to this point

the anarchists feel no threat, and John Sayles concentrates on their old relationships and how they've developed through the years. For most of the story it's a typical reunion without much happening, except for modestly detailed characterizations. We do come to know these characters.

But then comes the incident—an abrupt change—and now the story goes into high gear. The characterizations John Sayles gave earlier become the basis for what will happen, and we understand that this is the only way these people could respond. The tension rises immediately, the pace shifts and the scene blossoms in our imaginations because it is so dramatic.

Think of a group of septuagenarians, linking arms, sitting on the floor of a mid-town ballroom and singing the "Internationale" while an unctuous hotel manager rages with impotence.

That's drama and that's showing.

The effect of an incident is to create movement in some form, similar to the effect of characters moving on or off stage in the theatre. Movement is key in whatever we write because it avoids that deathly label of "stasis," which means, literally, *standing still* and is applied to a piece of work where nothing happens. I have had students roam through ten or fifteen pages of fiction and never have anything happening. Their story stands absolutely still. Characters may be talking, sensitive descriptions might be offered, but the story resembles dead weight.

That's what makes incidents so valuable. They can kick the story into action, get it moving, and with it will come the reader's attention and imagination. Author Robert Sheckley understands the need for movement, even though he might prefer to write without it. "I love to *write* soliloquy," he stated, "but I have noticed that I rarely like to read it." The problem with soliloquy is that *nothing happens*. It is a speech about things which may have happened, but while the speaker is speaking, there is no movement. It's clearest, of course, on the stage, where all action stops for the duration of the soliloquy. But translated to the written page, the same effect occurs. The action stops, and Sheckley is wise to know that his reaction is similar to most readers.

So what does he do?

"My eye looks for movement. I want something to be happening. I shy away from books with characters who spend a lot of time thinking about their feelings. The characters I like to read about are generally talking to somebody . . ."

And when characters are talking, that's dialogue, and we know the sense of drama can't be far behind. Even as characters converse, the opportunity for movement is there (and it doesn't have to be physical movement, either). They can argue (an incident), they can divulge a secret (an incident), they can discover things about one another (an incident), they can make a deal (an incident).

All we need is that three-word phrase—an abrupt change. Anything that brings this about is an incident, and movement is sure to follow.

One way to develop movement is by having the characters come together to discuss something of importance. Think back again to the theatre and recall how the action on stage grows more intense as more characters make their appearance, and events become focused. The same thing happens on the written page, and when the characters come together for some purpose, the reader's attention focuses. We want to know why the meeting, and we want to know what will happen.

The meeting, of course, is an incident, just as the entrance of the smiling manager was an incident in John Sayles's story. The meeting constitutes an abrupt change and gets things moving. Take a look at the way Bobbi Ann Mason handles it in her story, *Spence and Lila*, which takes place in a hospital. Lila has undergone a mastectomy, and her husband, Spence, and two daughters are worried about her, especially when she complains about pain in her neck. The doctors tell her they might have to operate again and they give her an angiogram. Most of the story takes place around Lila's hospital bed, and there is much dialogue, though almost no physical movement. Spence, however, gets up and walks out of the room and into the hallway. At this point Bobbi Ann Mason creates an incident:

> The surgeon arrives, in his green garb. Spence is relieved that Cat and Nancy aren't there to pounce on him.
>
> "We have the results of the angiogram," the doctor says, glancing at his clipboard. "She's sixty percent blocked on the left side and forty percent on the other one. My recommendation is to open up that artery on the left side and pull out that plaque, and then we see how well she does. I don't want to do them both at once because of her weakened condition. And there's a chance she'll do so well she won't need the other one done."
>
> The thought of opening an artery makes Spence picture skinning a snake. He tries to think of what to ask. "She complained about the dizziness in Florida," he says . . .

In theatrical terms we have shifted the scene from the hospital bed to the hallway and we have shifted the focus from family members around the hospital bed to Spence and the doctor. Two things are developed by this incident: Bobbi Ann Mason gives us information about Lila (which we haven't had before), and we feel a heightening of tension because now it's been confirmed that Lila is sicker than she or anyone else expected. The drama builds, and as it does we find ourselves visualizing Spence and the doctor in the hallway discussing what to do about Lila. Note how Bobbi Ann Mason shows us what is happening. She uses dialogue instead of straight narrative, and she has this information given to Spence outside Lila's hearing (which also contributes to tension-building because now we, the readers, know something one of the lead characters doesn't know).

This little incident draws a picture in clearest terms about Lila and her health and about Spence and her family and what they are going to have to cope with. It provides that abrupt change we seek, and our imaginations fill in the rest.

Many times we don't need to shift the scene in order to develop an incident. All we need do is shift a character's attention to something significant while the scene continues to play out. It's an easy thing to do:

  - a man and a woman are taking a walk and the man points to a soaring bald eagle about to pounce on unsuspecting prey
  - a woman is undergoing rigorous cross-examination in a courtroom. The door opens and an obese male shuffles in and waves at the witness

No scene shift here, only a change in focus. And it might be momentary, too, but long enough to beckon the reader's imagination and heighten his or her awareness.

That's one thing about incidents, they don't have to be long in duration. A few seconds could do it because the incident's purpose is to spark the reader's interest, and sometimes that doesn't take long. See how Peter Maas did it with his novel *Father and Son* about a successful businessman and his young son who becomes involved with the Irish Republican Army while attending Harvard University. One evening father (Michael), a widower, and son (Jamie) and Jamie's fiancée are at a Cambridge pub where

Kevin Dowd, an IRA man, appears. He has his eye on Jamie for some IRA work, though Jamie doesn't know it. Jamie has just asked his father if his fiancée could join them at their beach house after the end of the term, and Michael is torn between having Jamie to himself and sharing him.

> [Michael] looked away, and almost in relief he saw the man who was Kevin Dowd staring intently at them. "Jamie, do you know who that guy at the bar is, the one in the dark sweater?" and Jamie said, "I haven't a clue. I think I've seen him here once or twice before . . ."

The shift of attention to Kevin Dowd at the bar is an incident because it changes the focus of the conversation at the table where Michael will have to cope with the emotions of sharing his son. Now they can talk about the stranger at the bar, and even though this is a momentary diversion, it redirects the pace of the story. Though Jamie has never met Kevin Dowd, we know he has his eye on him, and we know that sooner or later they will meet. This quick reference to him in the barroom serves to foreshadow that future meeting as well as to increase the tension level. A moment before, the atmosphere was congenial around the table, but now a sinister note has crept in . . . and the reader should be caught by it.

Note two things: the scene hasn't shifted; the incident occurs in the barroom and no one has left; when the incident is over, the scene will remain the barroom. The incident is momentary in length, yet it does its job of grabbing the reader's interest and building tension into the story.

Here again, we have dialogue developing the incident, just as we had with Bobbi Ann Mason. Dialogue is a great drama-producer (we know that from Chapter Six), and when it's used with incident and to support the story, the reader knows a "happening" is taking place.

10

"Fictionalize" Your Nonfiction

When Norman Mailer wrote *The Executioner's Song* in 1979, he inserted an afterword:

"This book does its best to be a factual account of the activities of Gary Gilmore from April 9, 1976 . . . until his execution a little more than nine months later . . . This does not mean it has come a great deal closer to the truth than the recollections of the witnesses . . . *It is a factual account*, a true life story . . ."

Those of us who remember the saga of Gary Gilmore recall the wide attention devoted to whether a convicted murderer could demand to be executed for his crimes. This was no tale out of a novelist's fertile imagination. It actually happened, and Norman Mailer dramatized it in his book.

But he didn't offer it in standard *here are the facts* journalistic style. He called it a factual account, yet he applied some fiction technique and employed his novelist's skill. Here's a sample:

Gilmore brought the automatic to Jensen's head. "This one is for me," he said, and fired.

"This one is for Nicole," he said, and fired again. The body reacted each time.

He stood up. There was a lot of blood. It spread across the floor but at a surprising rate. Some of it got onto the bottom of his pants . . .

Mailer wasn't there when Gary Gilmore said these things, nor did he witness the spread of the blood, but he was probably informed about them when he did his interviewing or when he read police reports or other case reports. The point is that he took the facts and turned them into drama through injecting dialogue and by breaking the narrative into short, snappy sentences. He poured life into the scene.

What he did was to "fictionalize" the nonfiction.

Starting in the early 1960s stodgy old non fiction writing—*"the facts, ma'am, only the facts!"*—underwent a face lift when people like Tom Wolfe and Truman Capote began to take straight reportage and mix in fiction-writing techniques such as dialogue and foreshadowing and flashbacks. The idea was to create an art form out of truth and reality instead of from the four corners of the writer's imagination.

And it has worked. Norman Mailer certainly advanced things with his book about Gary Gilmore, and today non-fiction writing is much different from what it was a generation ago. The line of demarcation with fiction has blurred. While that has created other problems (such as the extent to which a writer should fictionalize, and what to call something that is essentially factual but has elements of re-creation), there is vividness in the nonfiction we now read.

Look no further than *Miami*, Joan Didion's book about

politics and internecine warfare among the Hispanics in the capital of Latin America, and the continuing relationship between them, the United States Government, Cuba and Central America. Here she discusses how Cuban exiles in Miami view Americans:

> Americans, above all, lacked "passion," which was the central failing from which most of these other national peculiarities flowed. If I wanted evidence that Americans lacked passion, I was advised repeatedly, I had only to consider their failure to appreciate *la lucha* [the struggle]. If I wanted further evidence that Americans lacked passion, I had only to turn on a television set and watch Ted Koppel's "Nightline," a program on which, I was told a number of times, it was possible to observe Americans "with very opposing points of view" talking "completely without passion," "without any gestures at all," and "seemingly without any idea in the world of conspiring against each other, despite being totally opposed."

These are the facts, of course, but note how she presents them, she injects herself into the discourse, using the first person, and she adds snippets of dialogue without specific attribution. We know that using the first person has the advantage of making the character more vulnerable to the reader because the reader is now privy to the character's thoughts and fears. The reader and the character come closer together because the writer has allowed the reader inside the character's head and thus the reader has become more involved in the story. The reader feels the drama, and the writer can sit back content.

Because there's showing, not telling.

The little portions of dialogue accomplish the same thing. Joan Didion arrays them, one after the other, as if they are rattled off in a crowd (they may well have been—

we don't know, but it's not really important because it is the words, themselves, we focus upon). There's drama in dialogue, as we've seen, and when Didion adds these snippets, she's building up the drama. She didn't have to do it that way, of course. She could have given identity to each commentator, she could have removed the quote marks and described the comments (such as: Americans were considered to be without passion because they didn't talk with gestures, and they had no interest in conspiring against one another merely because they didn't agree).

But putting quote marks around the comments adds drama, and when that happens, we know we're getting the reader's attention. Fiction writers work with dialogue and first person all the time, and there's no reason why nonfiction writers can't do the same thing.

The idea of using dialogue is central to building drama in our nonfiction writing. The question of how fabricated it should be and whether a note to the reader from the author about the extent of this fabrication is a moral issue that each writer must address. My own feeling is that readers have a *right* to know the genesis of the dialogue, and if there is fabrication, even though fairly slight, the author has a duty to make it known (because the reader trusts the author, and the author must have respect for the reader). But that doesn't mean dialogue shouldn't be fabricated—only that the reader be forewarned if it is.

Take Issac Bashevis Singer whose many works speak to the Jewish experience both as immigrants in America and in their homelands. In the foreword to *Lost In America*, he writes:

> This work does not pretend to be autobiographical . . . Because many of the people described are still alive . . . I could not tell the story of my life in the

usual style of a memoir . . . I had to skip dates as well as places . . . and I consider this work no more than fiction set against a background of truth . . .

And then he proceeds to relate a story in the first person, and he uses fiction-writing devices to make it more dramatic. He refuses to call it an autobiography, and he admits he has fabricated dates and places, and he also admits that certain characters are not portrayed as they really are. He calls the story fiction.

Yet it is set against a *background of truth*. To me, this means the underlying tale is nonfictional and he has taken dramatic license with characters, dialogue, time and setting. If the basic story wasn't true, why would he have bothered to refer to a background of truth? He was trying to be honest with us and show us that his story is not an imaginative romp, but a true-life tale with some fictional underpinning. In the book he is a young writer is Warsaw, Poland before the war, and in this passage he is calling his friend, Stefa, to see if a letter has come.

. . . I heard the ringing and, presently, Stefa's voice. Stefa had so utterly rejected the idea of assimilation that she often insisted on being addressed as Sheba Leah, and she called me Yitzchok, Itche, and sometimes even Itchele. She now exclaimed:

"Yitzchok, if you called me a minute before, no one would have answered! I went down to get a paper."

"What's the news?"

"Bad as always. But I have some good news for you. There is mail for you."

"From where?"

"From halfway around the world—from Paris, from New York, from the American consul. It seems there are two letters from New York. Shall I take a look?"

"We'll look together" . . .

Dialogue passages such as these fill the book, and it's obvious the author wasn't reproducing the words from a transcript of the conversation or from letters. He was relying upon his memory, but he was also relying upon his innate storytelling ability, which encouraged him to dramatize. Remember, he warned us . . . *I consider this work no more than fiction* . . . , and so we shouldn't be surprised that he might have fabricated some (or most) parts of the dialogue, as well as other portions of the story.

But look at what he has done with the nonfiction side of his tale. He has written in the first person, just as Joan Didion did with her story, and he has developed tension. Sheba tells him there is a letter, and because it is something he has been waiting for, we, the readers, get caught up in whether the letter will meet his expectations. We begin to empathize with him, and once we do that, we have identified with him.

And once we do that, we have involved ourselves in the story.

And it doesn't matter whether the story is true or not. We are being entertained.

It wouldn't have worked this way a generation ago. Nonfiction was fact oriented, and attempts to fictionalize portions met with frowns. The feeling, I suppose, was that calling something nonfictional meant it had to be totally accurate and truthful, and that once some fictional devices crept in, it wouldn't be long before the truth and accuracy might get shaky. But the sense of drama should permeate all types of writing, and the important thing, from a reader's point of view, is that there is interesting, exciting prose. Calling it fiction or nonfiction is important only to establish whether the writer is relating something he or she experienced or witnessed, or whether it is something from the imagination. The reader wants to know these things in order to feel closer to the writer and participate in the events on the page. But . . . the reader also wants to be entertained, and trying to fit any piece of writing into categories like fiction and nonfiction isn't of much interest so long as the writer is being honest.

Give me a story! says the reader.

Fiction or nonfiction? asks the writer.

Who cares? I want a story.

And so, in the past generation, we have developed hybrid literature which has been variously defined:

- "the nonfictional novel"—Truman Capote's *In Cold Blood*
- "a factual account, a true life story"—Norman Mailer's *The Executioner's Song*
- "fiction set against a background of truth"—Isaac Bashevis Singer's *Lost in America*
- "spontaneity of thought, not just speech"—Tom Wolfe's *The Right Stuff*

Each of the descriptions was used by the author about his own book, and each author generously dipped into fiction-writing techniques to put across the story of his essentially true account. What are some of these techniques?

Nonfiction writer Samm Sinclair Baker (*The Doctor Debitz Champagne Diet; Reading Faces*) described a conversation he had with a major book publisher:

"What makes a best-selling novel?" he asked.

"It must be a page turner," the publisher responded, adding that when readers got to the bottom of the page, the prose must *force* them to flip to the next. "That goes for anything you write," the publisher emphasized.

A page turner. Fiction *or* nonfiction. "[The publisher] went on to discuss some of the ABCs of writing fiction," Baker wrote, "including anecdotes, background, characters, dialogue. I decided to adapt those fiction essentials to produce nonfiction that would sell."

Anecdotes, background, characters, dialogue. Four fiction techniques that can be adapted to nonfiction. They all serve the same purpose—to dramatize the prose so it excites the reader and creates a word-picture in the reader's mind, so it *shows*, not tells. For example, in Chapter Eight we see how anecdotes can be woven into the text and add to drama and excitement because every reader wants a story, and anecdotes, more than anything else, are stories. Developing a nonfiction anecdote is no different from developing a fictional one, the only difference being the degree of fact one wants to portray. With nonfiction the anecdote must have actually happened, but where it's inserted and how it's used are part of the overall dramatic purpose.

Or take dialogue. From Joan Didion, Norman Mailer and Isaac Bashevis Singer, we've seen how it can be woven into factual text and will pep up the drama. Dialogue is a classic fiction technique, but there's no reason why it can't be used in nonfiction, also—provided it is an honest re-creation. As we've noted, some writers have fudged on this a bit, in the interests of drama, but then they have also warned the reader about what they did. An honest re-creation may be the best we can hope for because dramatic effect is what we seek, and a word-for-word rehash of exact dialogue will only succeed in putting readers to sleep. Dialogue and conversation are not the same, as discussed in Chapter Six, and a word-for-word rehash is conversation, not dialogue.

The list of fiction techniques that can be used with nonfiction goes on, however. Composite characterizations, for example. Many fictional characters are drawn from a number of sources as the writer blends bits and pieces of those he has known or read about with the images in his imagination. In nonfiction the composite character is also effective, and the advantage is that the character can be expanded or molded to serve a particular purpose. It's no mystery that a story with characters will intrigue a reader because of the personal-involvement factor, and any experienced writer will strive to "personalize" his or her story so there are characters for the reader to identify with. Here, again, we've developed drama, and if the character is a composite (that is, drawn from several sources), the drama isn't diminished.

For example, I co-authored a book on the art of ballet, *The Parents' Book of Ballet*, and we felt it was important to portray the young person whose parents would be reading the book. So we had a chapter, "The Lifestyle of the Teenaged Dancer," and here's the way we described the young dancer's bedroom at home:

> Sodden balls of lamb's wool fill the basket and bottles of floor wax shellac share a table with polyurethane floor sealer and tubes and jars of theatrical make-up. Blue rubber foot strengtheners lie on the bed amidst a pile of mutilated clothing . . . "What did you *do* to that pretty leotard I bought you last month!" The back's been cut and the front safety pinned, full-length parachute pants have been cut into shorts.
>
> "It lets me dance better."
>
> There's more. Tights have their feet cut out.
>
> "So I can wear them on my arms under a leotard," is the ready answer.
>
> Other tights have their foot-bottom seams cut open.
>
> "So I can fix up my feet if they blister . . ."

There was no single young dancer who lived exactly like this or said exactly these words, yet there was enough of *most* young dancers in the portrayal that readers could sense the characterization and imagine the scene. This was a composite characterization, yet it served a well-defined purpose: it illustrated the young dancer's obsession with her art, and it showed that in spite of pursuing an arduous, demanding career, the young dancer was still a teenager underneath with the messy room and the strange clothing concoctions.

And note the dialogue, too. An honest re-creation, actually, but typical and illustrative. We could have written all this in narrative, describing what the room looked like and what the young dancer did to her clothing to make it more appropriate for her needs. But doesn't the dialogue make it more of a story, and don't we get a mental image of the young dancer earnestly explaining why she did such bizarre things to her clothing? None of this would have been possible if we had stayed with the narrative, even though the point might have been made just as well.

But good nonfiction writing is more than simply making a point. It should entertain as it discourses, and through the use of dramatic techniques such as dialogue, composite characterizations and anecdotes, this will be done. If we carry the effort further, we could add to the list of fiction-writing techniques that might work with nonfiction:

- quick scene intercuts (providing tension)
- flashbacks (a fuller storyline and better reader involvement)
- interior monologue (closer reader identification with the character)

But whatever the technique, the key is this: think drama, think excitement. Nonfiction that *shows* instead of tells is what we're after.

11

Turn Narrative Into Excitement

Sometimes, it's amusing to hear critics complain about a writer whose work in a genre field (mystery, romance, western, horror) has rocketed to prominence: "he (or she) knows how to follow a formula, that's all."

As if it were like following directions on the back of a spaghetti carton.

"It's not literature, of course," they insist.

The world is made up of critics, as every writer knows, and many of them have little understanding of, or sympathy with, the writing process and what we try to achieve. Writing, to people such as this, is like the process of the stamping machine on an assembly line—*center the object, hit the button, stamp, stamp, stamp!* Out comes the little gem, to be admired and refinished and packaged and sold for $19.95.

And when the money flows back in, there's SUCCESS! . . . and some hard-held envy from those who witnessed and shook their heads and didn't participate. "It's not literature, folks, nothing cosmic to ponder or the kind of writing that will hang around for generations. Pop writing. Comes and goes with the seasons . . ."

Ah, these critics, holding us to such high standards, when, in truth, the writer's art encompasses far more and far less than what they suppose. For underlying all our achievements is a constant, and it doesn't matter whether we're struggling to produce "literature" or moving blocks around to produce generic fiction. What we seek is the *story*, and what we are is *storytellers*. Writers write *stories*!

That's our constant, and critics who complain about the form of our writing, or its appeal, cannot touch our writer's core, so long as the story works. That is how writers should be judged and should judge one another.

As storytellers we're part of a grand tradition that reaches to the earliest portions of recorded history. Through the story, people learned about who they were and where they came from, and the storytellers were crucial members of any ancient gathering. By the time of Homer and the Age of Greece, storytelling had become an art form that provided cultural underpinning and cohesion. Storytelling was a vital force.

It remains so today, and it retains much of its classic form. We've come to think of it as narrative. That is, the storyteller gives us narrative (even tough it might be spiced with dialogue) and calls it a story. The late William Sloane, a well-respected editor for many years, gave storytelling a key place in how we live:

> "Storytelling is the way a child learns the delight of the language, of the world of words, and of the bridge words build between people."

To him, storytelling was a narrator's art:

> "Narration is, indeed, an overwhelming large part of the daily dialogues we have with each other, and we exchange narrative anecdotes as a kind of game."

Think how narratives come up:

> "What's the story, son?"
> "A likely story!"

"I want a bedtime story . . ."

Narrative is the heart of storytelling, it is the way the human condition is displayed and enlarged upon; it is what sweeps us along. A writer must have a feel for narrative. As William Sloane writes, ". . . there is a special quality about a writer with the narrative gift. He makes you want to read on, to find out what is going to happen."

Narrative provides us *information*, and it does so in storytelling fashion, entertaining us as we go. Good narrative has drama, and that is what intrigues us and keeps us glued to the page. Where the drama slips away, the narrative becomes lecture instead of storytelling, and the reader loses that all-important word-picture.

But narrative *with* drama . . . ah, that's showing not telling.

There are ways we can do this, certain techniques which can be learned and used. The point is to get away from explanations and lengthy recitations where there really is no story. One of the more obvious techniques is to inject tension into the narrative, to develop some type of emotional or physical conflict. See the way Nathanael West did it with his short novel, *The Dream Life of Balso Snell* which is a journal of a self-professed lyric poet who shows some of his verse, some of his inner thoughts, some of his life experiences in a modified form of stream-of-consciousness writing. He hears of the death of his friend, Saniette, and he contemplates his reaction:

> The inevitability of death has always given me plea-
> sure, not because I am eager to die, but because all the
> Saniettes must die. When the preacher explained the
> one thing all men could be certain of—all must die—
> the king of France became angry. When death pre-
> vailed over the optimism of Saniette she was, I am
> certain, surprised. The thought of Saniette's surprise
> pleases me, just as the king's anger must have pleased

the preacher . . . Only a portion of my dislike for Saniette is based on the natural antipathy pessimists feel for optimists . . .

This narrative goes on for three and one-half pages without dialogue or change in point of view or other break in the narrative flow. We stay with the narrator throughout, and we get caught up in relationship with Saniette even though she has appeared before in the book and is certainly no mystery now. But—we do learn some new things about her (and about the narrator and their relationship), and we feel a sense of identity.

Two things are at work here: first there is the tension. In the final sentence we find out that the narrator didn't like Saniette (even though they had lived together at one time), and this brings in the element of conflict which is the basis for tension. But there's more tension too: in the first sentence the narrator gloats that death gives him pleasure and that all the Saniettes in the world will eventually die . . . thus each death renews his pleasure (and isn't there conflict over the fact that death in one person provides pleasure to another?). Let's take the tension even further . . . West describes the king of France's anger over the preacher's advice that he, too, will die. Anger is conflict, it's emotional contention, and it brings tension into the story. The fact that the preacher was pleased by the king's anger—and the fact that the narrator was pleased by Saniette's surprise and disintegration of optimism—are still other tension producers.

All of these things in one short selection, all of them developing tension. That's the way we build drama into our narrative.

But there's a second technique at work here, as well (something already explored in Chapter Nine). Since good narrative is storytelling, we should try to develop the elements of a story within the narrative. Nathanael West has done this here. His little incident between the king of France and the preacher does the trick, and even though it's only a couple of lines, it does offer a quick dramatic scene for the reader to ponder. Think of the word-picture: The king, self-absorbed, unchallenged, thoroughly powerful, and his preacher, who informs him (probably with some trepidation) that he is no different from any other mortal—he will die, too. And the king's anger erupts at this effrontery, while the preacher probably quakes.

But, then, secretly, we learn the preacher was pleased by the king's anger, and we might guess it's because the king has retreated to mere mortality (which means the preacher has discovered a level of power over the king).

Here, then, is a little incident within the broader confines of a lengthy narrative passage, and what makes it particularly eyecatching for us is that it injects drama into the narrative, it provides something for the reader to imagine and identify with. Narrative which can include an incident or two will avoid the "dullness" label so many attach to exposition. Try this little exercise:

Take a hobby or some process that's familiar and not too complicated. Explain how it works, in step-by-step fashion and try to make it as clear as possible.

Now, think of a threat to this hobby or process that might damage or destroy it, and describe how this threat might erupt, and then describe how the narrator feels about the threat and its consequences.

Then, have the threat happen . . .

By following these steps there would be drama in the narrative because we've done the two things that Nathanael West did: we developed tension and we created an incident. A narrative of exposition becomes a narrative with drama, *and we still don't lose the exposition*!

That's the interesting side of it. We turn a lecture into a show, but the information stays, and the reader is not only entertained but also informed.

I recall a conversation with my agent years ago when I was much newer at the writer's trade. My wife and I had the elements of a manuscript about the war crimes trial of the Norwegian traitor, Vidkun Quisling (whose name appears in most dictionaries as synonymous with "traitor) and the way some of the evidence had been gathered. We had access to documents which showed how close the Allies came to botching Quisling's prosecution, and we had a transcript of the trial (which had never been released to the general public). The problem was setting the scene so that the courtroom drama could develop. It meant long stretches of narrative about the search for the evidence, how teams of Norwegian investigators had scoured the European continent and the captured German archives for the documents which connected Quisling to the Nazis. All that narrative bothered me, and I mentioned it to the agent (for whom this would be our first piece of work).

"Trials make a good story," she said.

"There's a lot of exposition to write," I said. "We have to explain what they were doing and how they found the evidence, step by step."

"Trials sell well."

"The trial is only *part* of the story," I said.

"Did they go searching for evidence?"

"That's the exception."

"That's the story," she said.

She saw right away that the narrative portion could be as exciting as the trial itself because it contained a classic tension-builder, a search for something important. Will it be found or won't it, can it help or can't it? The characters rush against time, and we don't know whether they will succeed until the end. Figuratively, we hold our breaths.

In addition, the search, itself, was made up of little incidents, stories within stories, as one stop led to a clue or two and then to another stop where more clues might be uncovered. As the narrative progressed and the search continued, the incidents became the story, and the drama was heightened because things were happening.

Incidents do that in a narrative—they provide excitement by presenting things that happen, and the reader is drawn in because he or she wants to know what the outcome will be.

"I see what you mean," I said to the agent.

I had learned the importance of developing incidents within narrative in order to build excitement and drama. Simply put, it's good writing technique.

See how novelist Craig Nova did it in *The Congress-man's Daughter*, a story of small town life. His narrator describes the town, using the first person, and mentions the shops, roads, buildings. He talks of a young woman named Sally who came from across the river and found a job in a local factory where spark plugs were made. Then, continuing the narrative:

It's gone now, but when Sally worked there she found a young man and got pregnant. Or maybe there was more than one young man, and she didn't know who the father really was, or didn't care. She had her child, a little girl, and lived alone with her in an apartment in a building by the river. Or tried to. I'm amazed she held out as long as she did, since the women of the town, those who organized the garden parties to benefit the museum and library, the women of advanced ideas, those who canvassed for the right candidates and who gave money to the right causes, those women hounded her . . .

He stays with Sally's story a bit longer and then turns to other things, all the while continuing in first person and continuing with narrative. In fact, the entire narrative passage here runs more than seven pages, and not once does the author use dialogue or quotes. At its conclusion we have come to know the town intimately, understanding its physical layout and its soul.

Seven pages is a long stretch of narrative to keep the reader's interest, but Craig Nova carries it off with techniques such as the use of incidents and the story about Sally. The moment he personalized the narrative by bringing in Sally (up to this point he had been describing physical character of the town), he gave the reader a peg on which to hang a sense of identity. It's hard to get emotionally involved with buildings and streets and businesses, but not so with people. The fact that Sally had a difficult time in town only adds to the poignancy of the portrayal and makes us all feel sympathy for her. Once we feel the sympathy, of course, we've identified with the character.

But note, too, that the entire narrative passage, all seven pages, concerns much more than Sally and what happened to her. It covers other subjects, though no other incident. But, often, it takes only one incident to spice up a lengthy narrative passage because the reader's imagination will linger on the story running through the narrative even while taking in the information it imparts. The incident acts as a conduit for the rest of the narrative, and the reader's interest won't fall away.

The key to good narrative writing is to make it interesting. Not a profound thought, really. But examine what I mean. I mean—*interesting*! I mean shoulder-grabbing, attention-getting prose. I mean dramatic, exciting.

I mean using those writing skills that work with generic fiction: mystery, suspense, horror, erotic and so forth. We don't have to *write* a generic fiction story to use these techniques in a narrative passage and generate interest. We don't even have to develop them far, only hint at their application. The point is that readers will respond when elements like these are part of the narrative. For example, in a narrative about the soil and ground cover of the desert southwest, a brief reference to buried Indian tombs and the vengeful spirits which protect them would probably get the reader's attention.

Or a description of a run-down, seedy section of town might digress to a certain motel and the fact that one room was kept aside for "special" customers who enjoyed particularly innovative sex games, and then might further digress to the night of a police raid where a self-righteous chief of detectives was occupying the special room, and then back to more description of the town.

We want to infiltrate the narrative with these generic fiction techniques because they *are* drama-producing, they exist to present dramatic situations. See what Edith Wharton did a number of years ago with a narrative passage in *The Age of Innocence*, her book about New York society near the turn of the century. Newland Archer, soon to marry, meets Countess Olenska, an American woman recently divorced from a European, and the Countess invites him to call at her rented townhouse, which he does, only to find that she is out. But the maid says she will return shortly, and he decides to wait in the drawing room. At this point the narrative passage begins, and Newland Archer thinks about his upcoming marriage and honeymoon, how his fiancée would furnish this townhouse if they were to live in it, about the Italian art that is displayed. And then he senses there is something different in this drawing room, in the way it is furnished:

> He had before been in drawing rooms hung with red damask, with pictures 'of the Italian school'; what struck him was the way in which Medora Monson's shabby hired house with its blighted background of pampas grass and Rogers statuettes had, by a turn of the hand, and the skillful use of a few properties been transformed into something intimate, 'foreign', subtly suggestive of old romantic scenes and sentiments. He tried to analyze the trick, to find a clue to it in the way the chairs and tables were grouped . . .

This passage goes on for four pages without dialogue of any kind. What Edith Wharton has done is to turn straight description into a little mystery, forcing her character to wonder how something happened even as he searches the room and we get a full description. She has him looking for a "trick" in the decor, and this can't help but gain our interest. All of us are intrigued by mysteries, and while this one certainly has no dead bodies or shattering suspense, it does present a riddle or enigma. What was it about that room that made it so appealing and intimate? What did it tell about the woman who was renting the house? In time, of course, we'll get the answers, but through this narrative passage, the puzzle lingers on.

And so does our interest. Edith Wharton has taken a page from the mystery-writers' manual by setting up the puzzle and not providing a quick answer, and in the process she has made reading the narrative passage agreeable. The puzzle or the mystery creates drama by plucking our interest, not in the character of Newland Archer, particularly, but in the solution to why the room was so intimate. We want to know, and Wharton, like any good writer, strings us along while making sure we take in the other portions of the narrative.

Think generic fiction in situations like this—but don't think too intensely. A dab will do fine.

12

Steady on the Pacing

Some years ago I worked up courage to try long fiction. I had written short stories and brief sketches (some of which had actually been published), but the prospect of producing something that might run 250–300 pages seemed daunting. How could I sustain a story of that length, how could I persevere for the months it would take?

Do it! my adventurous side urged.

Stay with what you know, my safe side responded. Polish a skill you already have.

But the story idea was too strong to put aside, and I knew I'd always regret not having tried.

I wish I could say the story idea became a book which was swept up by a publisher and turned into a raging success; such a fantasy is the elixir we writers thirst for. But the truth is the manuscript was never published (for reasons which have nothing to do with this chapter), yet in the writing I discovered things which have sustained me ever since, regardless of whether the story I'm writing is short or long.

What I found was the importance of pace to any story, how vital it is for an even flow which will then retain the reader's attention. Agitate the pace of a story, and the reader will feel jerked around, may even sense the author's lack of interest in his or her reaction. I discovered that pace has a double application.

When I began to write that book-length manuscript, I didn't have to cope with weeks between writing sessions; I was able to write every day. The result was that, suddenly, I had fifty pages, then seventy-five pages, and I realized I had never written anything so long. And there was a rhythm and a flow to the way I wrote. I was in a groove. Before page one hundred, however, I had to leave my daily writing schedule because of a family emergency, and it was about three weeks before I tried to resume.

And that's when I discovered something I'll call *procedural* pacing. Because when I picked up my story, I found I had lost the flow. I could not recapture the daily page output because I no longer felt a part of the story. I reread what I had already written, but it didn't propel me with the same gusto. Somehow, the story had come to a dead end. I could still produce the pages, but what I was now writing had only tenuous connection to what I had already produced, there was no groove any longer. The procedural side of my pacing was out of synch, and piling up the pages meant nothing.

While I wrestled with all of this, I came upon *substantive* pacing, that is, the pacing inherent in *what* we write, not *how* we write—the content of our work. I discovered that when I resumed writing after three weeks, I had lost the sense of drama. I found myself falling back on exposition and undramatic narrative. I suppose I wanted to catch up the threads of the story again, and I began to write as if I had to make up for lost time. And so the drama in the first portion of the book became blunted when I tried to continue.

What had been showing became telling, and the pace of the entire book changed. *Substantive* pacing needs steadiness so the story moves with an even flow, so the drama can be developed naturally. I had lost the touch for that.

Procedural pacing, of course, has no direct effect on whether we're showing or telling, but what it does is establish a floor which develops the show or tell potential in *substantive* pacing. Casual, uneven writing sessions make it that much more difficult to pick up story threads and maintain them over a lengthy period. If the story contains a rising level of suspense, we have to pace it carefully, dropping small hints here and there, and slowly crafting the menace so the reader senses the growing tension until it explodes at the proper time. But if we write a few pages this week, then go back a month from now and do a few more, then do a couple a week later, then write steadily for four days, we could find our writing herky-jerky. Pacing is a subtle mechanism, and it must be coddled and understood. Our writing schedule must maintain a drum-beat regularity. Steady on the writing sessions means steady *potential* for the writing content.

Many of us have heard those dreaded words, "This story is out of control . . ." The writer has lost the handle on pacing, and the story bumps off in strange directions without a tie to what's gone on before it. A writer who spends too much time on exposition in the early portion of a story will then be forced to rush through the more dramatic portions, thus losing control of the way those dramatic portions should be presented. A writer who introduces a character mid-way through may have to devote major space to weaving that character into the story and placing his or her background in context before the story, itself, will move forward. This pause might be necessary so readers will relate to the character, but it could come at the expense of story movement and drama. It might have been better to have introduced the character earlier, before the pacing was established, or to have dropped hints about the character at several stages, instead of bunching everything at once.

Pace can always be changed. BUT . . . the change must be for a reason (sudden tension, character portrayal, passage of time). The writer must know why the pace is changing and how it's being accomplished. A writer who is aware of these things is a writer who is in control of his or her story.

But there can be too much story control, too. It's what E.S. Creamer calls "heavy-handed" writing, using a bullying approach with the reader. Heavy-handed prose often results in telling and not showing, and he describes it as: ". . . ungainly through unnecessary description, clumsy through repetition, tyrannical in ordering the readers around instead of allowing them the kind of creative leaps that make reading such a pleasure."

Overwriting is what he's referring to, and it's easy to see how this will affect pacing and a sense of drama. The flow is broken and nothing has been left to the imagination. "The key to avoiding heavy-handedness," Creamer informs us, "lies in what you leave out, not what you leave in."

Encourage the reader to make that creative leap, he is saying, make the reader a partner is story movement, not simply a backboard to bounce things off.

See how Katherine Mansfield does it with her short story, *The Fly*, where the elderly owner of a small factory has just been reminded of his son's death in World War I by the visit of a former employee. When he is alone, the owner recalls his deep grief and realizes how agitated he is now at being reminded about it. His eye suddenly catches a fly which had fallen into an inkwell and struggled out onto blotting paper. The owner drops another blob of ink on the fly and then another until he finally succeeds in killing it. The final two paragraphs in the story show masterful pacing:

> The boss lifted the corpse on the end of the paper knife and flung it into the wastepaper basket. But such a grinding feeling of wretchedness seized him that he felt positively frightened. He started forward and pressed the bell for Macey.
>
> "Bring me some fresh blotting paper," he said, sternly, "and look sharp about it." And while the old dog padded away, he fell to wondering what it was he had been thinking about before. What was it? It was . . . He took out his handkerchief and passed it inside his collar. For the life of him he could not remember.

Only in these closing paragraphs do we get a full view of the owner, even though he's been the protagonist throughout. But now we see him as he really is: old, forgetful, mean and probably senile. Up to this point he is portrayed as competent and clearly in charge of his company and his surroundings, and we build sympathy for him because of his grief for his dead son. By the end of the story, however, we have a cruel, unkind old man for whom it is hard to find any sympathy. Until the last few paragraphs, however, we had no hint whatsoever that he was really like this. The story pace was steady as the author built up sympathy for her character, and only in the final paragraphs, when she changes her pace, do we change our sentiments. By leaving out the unpleasant side of the owner's character until the end, she allows us to make the creative leap that E.S. Creamer mentioned, and we come up feeling sympathy for the character. Then, when she wished to spotlight the owner as he really is, she doesn't tell us he's mean and senile. She shows us by the way he kills the fly, by the way he treats Macey (thinking of him as "an old dog"), by the fact that in the span of a few short seconds he cannot remember the grief that had been so vivid in his mind. The author never tells us the owner is senile, but by allowing us to watch his thought processes, she shows us.

And note how the story would have suffered if the incident at the end had been worked in earlier. The steady pace of rising sympathy for the owner would have stopped abruptly. The change in pace showing the owner's senility would have brought a story climax but with major portions of the story still to go. And, in any case, what good purpose would there have been to insert the story climax in the middle?

None, of course, and so the steady pacing would have been shattered.

There is more to pace, however, than broad stretches of prose and chapter-by-chapter analysis. Sometimes it can be important to narrow our focus to individual paragraphs, sentences, even single words. Pacing—or more accurately, *changes* of pacing—must be considered here, too. James Kilpatrick, the well-known newspaper columnist, compared writing pace to the demands on the long-distance runner. It's ". . . the business of knowing when to slow down, when to speed up," he wrote. "Sentence length is one of the elements of pace. Syllabication is another . . . Voice is another element—active in one case, passive in the other. Simple sentences make a sprint; compound and complex sentences serve the mile run."

Sentence length, syllabication, verb voice . . . These operate to maintain pace *or* to change it. Keep them uniform and the pace remains steady; vary them (for good reason) and the pace will change. Let's look at sentence length, for example. A series of short, snappy sentences will tend to keep tensions and attention high because the effect is similar to an insistent drum roll. A series of compound sentences will tend to slow things down because everything is elongated and smoother. See the difference:

The sky opened. Rain hammered his car roof. Oncoming headlights blinded him. Sounds from other cars were mushy, indistinct. The smell from the back seat gagged him . . .

The sky opened and the rain hammered the car roof. Oncoming headlights blinded him while sounds from other cars seemed mushy, indistinct. But the smell from the back seat hovered, it brought bile to his mouth . . .

In the first selection, the short sentences push the drama level up, creating a sense of rising tension. In the second selection, the drama level is more sedate, and the tension level is lower. But in both cases the pace is steady. As far as it goes this is good. In a short space—a few lines or a couple of paragraphs—uniform sentence length can influence drama well, and the two examples show this. But extend these examples and their uniform sentence lengths for a page or more, and the uniformity becomes uninspiring because the sameness is now the rule rather than the exception. What had been showing for a few lines now becomes telling when the few lines become several paragraphs and more. Drama loses a great deal when it becomes too predictable.

So we vary pace sometimes in order to keep the drama flowing (recognizing, or course, that *steady* pacing must include *changes* of pace). Note how Ed McBain does it with *Vespers*, one of his 87th-Precinct novels. A priest has been murdered, and Detective Carella discovers that the priest had been deeply troubled by something he finally shared with his sister. Carella asks the sister about it and she responds:

". . . As I said, he was starting to get a bit hysterical by then. Because he was coming to what the *real* problem was, and it didn't have a damn thing to do with any of the *little* things he was talking about. It had to do with . . ."

A woman.

Her brother is involved with a woman.

He does not tell Irene how this started or even how long it has been going on, but it is tormenting him that he has violated his vows of chastity and trapped himself in a situation from which there is no escape. He loves Jesus Christ and he loves this woman and the two loves are incompatible and irreconcilable. He mentions that he has considered suicide . . .

Here, Ed McBain has made a double change of pace, from compound sentences in one paragraph to a two-word non-sentence, to a simple sentence . . . and then back to a compound sentence. All in the space of less than a page. The abruptness of the changes catches our attention, and we can feel the drama emerging because we are being given important information (it is, in fact, key information because it will explain the motive for the murder). Yet even as he changes pace here, Ed McBain maintains a steady forward movement in the story. (This excerpt appears on page 132—roughly forty percent through the book). He is describing things we haven't learned before and so another piece of the story puzzle is added. And he hasn't bunched the information at the beginning where it might interfere with the developing plot.

The important thing to remember about steady pacing is that while uniformity in sentence length, syllabication and verb voice might work well for a short time, their importance and impact will diminish when story movement is considered. Steady pacing in story movement (that is, overall story *development*) is what we should seek, and if we're successful, the need to bunch up narration or exposition in order to plug story holes will evaporate.

Think of story pacing the way a fine chef thinks of making a classic sauce: the procedure cannot be rushed, ingredients should be applied judiciously and with an eye towards the final result, the mixture should be stirred tenderly and over a uniform flame.

And the product should be tasted continually to assure solid effect.

In short, be aware of pace at all times, *procedural* (writing schedule) and *substantive* (writing content). Understand how and when it can go awry. As the chef drops condiments in his sauce, so the writer should drop in story tidbits at *planned points,* understanding the effect they will have and why:

- identify the most important scenes in the story and decide the crucial information to insert
- don't bunch up problems in one scene, stttrreeettcchhh them out
- think progressively—information should come in steps, building to a story climax

And when it comes to the information, think in terms of indirection. Hint at things, force the reader to make that creative leap, to figure things out for himself/herself. "Sentiment is best revealed indirectly, through detail rather than overt statement," E.S. Creamer believes. "Instead of describing how a character feels about death, the end of a romance, a thrill or a glimmer of happiness, set up the situation, then say how the character feels about the wallpaper, the sitcom on the television, the rustle of leaves."

This is the way we show and create drama. Keeping it under control and moving it forward steadily is the way we keep it dramatic.

And the way we keep our readers.

13

Keep Those Characters Alive!

"The reader reads fiction more for its people than for any other element, whether plot, setting or shock value," wrote the late editor William Sloane. He should know. He reviewed and edited thousands of manuscripts and spent his entire professional life as editor, publisher and writer. "Readers associate characters in fiction with their own lives and with their own experience. They will even name their children after fictional characters."

Reality and fiction are never so closely entwined for us as when we're dealing with characterization. It isn't only the sense of identity we feel, it's the fact that characters—people—are what give a story life. "Dead characters make dead prose . . ." is the way a former writing teacher of mine expressed it, and he was really offering the obvious: what possible interest could there be in a story where the characters were lifeless and dull? The reader *wants* to identify, and if the characters are dull or flat, interest will die away.

Of course, there are types of stories where characterization is less important than plot or setting—erotica, for example, or action-adventure—but in general literature, the characterizations must be sturdy and lifesize in order to keep the story going. For example, think of Uriah Heep, or Othello, or Simon Legree; they played such an important role in story development that it would be unthinkable to recast events without them. Yet being important to the story is not the whole answer. Characters must vibrate with life on the page, they must breathe and have substance.

Then readers can feel a part of the scene and the story. They "associate" the way they live with the way the characters live.

How do we develop characters like this? We strive to "show" such characters to the reader instead of "telling" the reader about them.

- a character doesn't like women and bullies them with regularity
- a character doesn't like women but we find out his mother dropped him in a trash can shortly after his birth and he was bullied by a foster sister

In the first selection we get no motivation, only a series of direct actions. If the action is strong enough, it might catch a reader sufficiently so the reader doesn't mind the superficiality of the characterization. But if the bullying is offered *without explanation,* and the action is not racehorse intense, the reader will turn away.

The reason is motivation. We need to know *why!* Otherwise the character remains a cypher, and the reader remains uninvolved.

So we turn to the second selection, and we see that here is motivation. Now we know why, and now we come to understand the character more easily. His bullying of women is a direct product of the brutalizing he received from women as a child. Motivation is one of the things that can add life and breath to a character because readers *understand,* and while they may not approve the underlying action, they can see logic in the cause and effect.

And this is how the reader becomes involved in the story. By understanding . . . by sympathizing . . . and now the character is alive!

All characters have a past, and it's the writer's job to make that past both interesting and germane to what is happening in the present. The more we know about a character, the more we'll understand the *why* questions. Motivation is only a part of the equation, but it does let us see into the character's past. But we should be able to go even further because a character's past is more than a feeder trough for motivation—it also provides general information that will fill in the portrait. Take a character who suffered from an alcoholic, abusive parent:

- motivation for sharp anger towards anyone who drinks might stem from this, as would a fear that he himself might follow in the alcoholic parent's footsteps
- the character's general past might include a loving aunt who offered comfort from the alcoholic abuse; might describe schooling adventures; might speak of first loves and first friends; might provide the details of the first year of his current marriage . . .

None of the items in the second selection need be motivators for what happens in the book. They simply fill in blanks about the character and give him body and depth. The first selection, of course, deals with motive, and while it also provides some information about the character, it is necessarily limited. If we portray our character fully, we are going to want to add some things about the character's past—things which may have nothing to do with motivation, but which offer a fuller portrait. We're going to want to do this because the reader will demand it, if we have succeeded in making our character interesting! Readers want to know more and more about interesting characters, just as we want to know more and more about interesting people we meet in real life.

So we fill in the blanks in our character's past, and readers find more and more to identify with. Understanding motivation is certainly one reason for doing this, but giving a character body is important, too, and characters live on the page when we give them substance, when we portray their pasts, *regardless of how it affects motivation.*

"To fully realize a character, however, you must give him a whole life *from the start,*" writes novelist Orson Scott Card. "He has a past, an elaborate set of meaningful connections to other people: family, friends, enemies, teachers, employers." Some of these will influence motivation in the story, but others will fill in background only. It is the writer's job to weave the two together so that the reader comes to *know* the character and feel a sense of identity. Or in William Sloane's words, so the reader comes to "associate" with the character.

This is the essence of "showing" instead of telling. A character who comes alive on the page is the product of dramatic inspiration, and this is what affects the reader. Giving a character a past so motivation and a fuller background can be portrayed is one key to unlock the door.

Take a look at Grace Paley's short story, *Friends,* which looks at the relationship of three women, Ann, Susan, the narrator, and their friend, Selena, who is dying of cancer. The three women have made a visit to Selena and now they discuss her and their own lives:

> Now, why are you taking all those hormones? Susan had asked Selena a couple of years earlier. They were visiting New Orleans. It was Mardi Gras.
>
> Oh, they're mostly vitamins, Selena said. Besides, I want to be young and beautiful. She made a joking pirouette.

Susan said, that's absolutely ridiculous.

But Susan's seven or eight years younger than Selena. What did she know? Because: People *do* want to be young and beautiful. When they meet in the street, male or female, if they're getting older, they look at each other's face a little ashamed. It's clear they want to say, Excuse me, I didn't mean to draw attention to mortality and gravity all at once . . .

Here is a characterization that springs to life, not through racehorse prose or through an emotional outpouring but in the simplest of ways: the dramatization of an eternal truth. *Everyone wants to be young and beautiful* says author Grace Paley, including Selena who now must face the devastation of her body through cancer. There's poignant irony to all this . . . Selena wants (or wanted) youth and beauty and what she got was the opposite, yet we see her motivation through the taking of hormones. The author might simply have told us that Selena wanted youth and beauty and that could have been enough to portray Selena. The eternal truth could act as a given without being mentioned. But its application is underscored when Grace Paley discusses it, and this has the effect of adding motivation to the other characters, Susan included. *Everyone wants to be young and beautiful.*

So motivation exists for Susan, Ann, and the narrator, too.

There's more. We get background on Selena and Susan here. For example, Susan is seven or eight years younger than Selena, and this limits her knowledge of what could motivate Selena; both Susan and Selena traveled to New Orleans a couple of years earlier and Selena was taking "vitamin" pills. Not all of this will provide motivation for subsequent acts, feelings or statements, but at least we get a clearer portrait of both women.

And that's the point. Is it hard to imagine Selena doing a

pirouette *after* she discloses that she is taking the pills and wants to be young and beautiful? Doesn't her twirl fit neatly with her need for youth and beauty? *This is what I'm going to look like,* she seems to be saying, *I'm young and dramatic and exciting* . . .

Note, too, the subtle tension between the two women. We know that tension is a drama builder, and here it works to develop character as well. Susan calls Selena's urge for youth and beauty "ridiculous," and Grace Paley adds that she really doesn't know much. But the contrast between Susan and Selena provides a dramatic touch that shows us the character of both women. They live on the page because we've come to understand them.

Obviously, a character must have some features which allow us to remember him or her, if there is to be any sense of identification. In terms of the writer's trade, characters have to be *memorable* to have impact on the reader. There must be something special about them, perhaps something unique or unusual, so the reader can develop a word-picture with which he or she can then associate. Once a character becomes memorable, there's life on the written page. Take a look at these fictional characters and note what makes them stick out:

- Jim, the runaway slave, in *The Adventures of Huckleberry Finn*—his wit and wisdom in spite of his lack of formal education
- Dorian Grey, in Oscar Wilde's *The Picture of Dorian Grey*—the character never ages, only his portrait does
- Spenser, the private investigator, in the books by Robert Parker—his excellent cooking skills while he follows a violent profession in a violent world
- Isadora Wing in Erica Jong's *Fear of Flying*—her search for perfect physical love in a non chauvinist world

Each of these characters has or does something that makes them stick out, and we relate to this. That doesn't mean we have to approve or disapprove, only that we *remember*. A character with a deadly violent temper might not please our sensibilities, but we're certainly aware of who that character is and how he or she fits into the book. We sense the tension whenever that character appears in a scene, and we carry a sense of foreboding that . . . something will happen!

This character is alive!

Or, perhaps, it is a character with a physical blemish, such as a birthmark or a wooden leg or a withered arm. In Ernest Hemingway's *The Sun Also Rises* it was impotence that plagued Jake Barnes; in Tom Robbins's *Even Cowgirls Get the Blues* it was Sissy's oversized thumb that kept us reading.

These are the things that make characters memorable, and once they become memorable, they live for us. Anything unusual, out of the ordinary, under the circumstances of the plot and setting, will do. For example, if the action takes place in a prisoner of war camp, then physical disabilities could abound and so a memorable physical characteristic would not be so unusual. But this might be a time for an *emotional* characteristic such as cowardice, something which sets this character apart from the others. We'll remember this character, not because he's to be applauded but because he's to be pitied.

On the other hand, there are times when the more grotesque the character, the more we'll remember him or her. In Edgar Allan Poe's *Berenice,* the narrator is betrothed to his niece, Berenice, a vivacious, outgoing woman. The narrator is her opposite, quiet, inner-looking and suffering from a mind-altering disease. Then Berenice becomes ill, and one evening the narrator is in his study and Berenice walks in on him. He has not seen her for a few days, and he doesn't realize how physically severe her illness has become:

> The forehead was high, and very pale, and singularly placid; and the once jetty hair fell partially over it, and overshadowed the hollow temples with innumerable ringlets, now of a vivid yellow, and jarring discordantly, in their fantastic character, with the reigning melancholy of the countenance. The eyes were lifeless, and lustreless, and seemingly pupilless, and I shrank involuntarily from their glassy stare to the contemplation of the thin and shrunken lips. They parted, and in a smile of peculiar meaning, the *teeth* of the changed Berenice disclosed themselves to my view. Would to God that I had never beheld them, or that, having done so, I had died! . . .

Note the memorable *physical* characteristics Poe describes:

- a pale forehead
- hollow temples
- melancholy countenance
- eyes, lifeless, lustreless, pupilless
- a glassy stare
- thin and shrunken lips
- terrorizing *teeth*

None of these individually might be enough to make the character memorable, but taken together they present a grotesque portrait (especially when we get to the teeth, which the author describes later and which form a key element in the plot). The fact that Berenice has changed from a beautiful young woman to a lifeless robot spurs the interest of the reader because we want to know *why,* as was our query when it came to motivation. Here we want to know why Berenice is like this and what will happen to her. In fact, it may well be that Berenice is little more than an apparition, that she has already died. Certainly when we examine her physical characteristics we could come to that conclusion. Read them again . . . couldn't a corpse have the same appearance?

And if Berenice is one of the walking dead, doesn't that make her memorable? There aren't many characters like this in literature, and Poe is clever enough to keep our attention focused on what makes her grotesque. From a technical writing viewpoint, note the adjectives Poe uses to build up the grotesque portrait: *hollow . . . lifeless . . . lustreless . . . pupilless . . . glassy . . . shrunken . . .* Each provides an image that contributes to the whole portrait, and taken together they create a memorable character.

This is "showing," or course. If Poe had decided to "tell," he wouldn't have gone into the image-producing adjectives, nor would he have tried to present Berenice in such a grotesque manner. He might have described her as looking pale and sickly, feeling uninterested in life and changed from the character she used to be. No images here, nothing *memorable* about her.

But Poe was too wise for that. He wanted Berenice to live for the reader—and that's exactly what happened.

Intimate details of a life are yet another way to fill out a character's dimensions on the page. Most of us are a bit nosey about how other people live (especially well-known people; witness the success of the weekly tabloids), and those intimate tidbits give us a sense of knowing and understanding that person just a bit more. It works the same way in literature: something intimate about a character will spark interest in the reader because the reader *knows* intuitively that most other characters in the book wouldn't have the same information. So the reader is privy to a sometime secret, even if it is on a fictional level, and that's generally pleasing.

Our creative minds can develop any number of characters and an intimate detail or two (think of Tolstoi's *Anna*

Karenina and the quiet love affair with Count Vronsky), and the more details we provide the more the reader will be intrigued. That's because we're developing a character who will be full of life on the page, and as we know, that's what readers enjoy.

Intimacy in a character's life might run from unkind feelings towards their children or parents to sexual practices and experiences to crimes committed or witnessed or planned to individual personal or work habits—anything, in fact, that is revealed to only a few.

Take a look at this selection from Philip Roth's *The Ghost Writer*. Young author, Nathan Zuckerman, having recently been published for the first time seeks out E.I. Lonoff, a distinguished author, for help and guidance. As they discuss the craft of writing, Lonoff launches into the way *he* approaches it:

> Meanwhile, he was saying to me, "I turn sentences around. That's my life. I write a sentence and then I turn it around. Then I look at it and I turn it around again. Then I have lunch. Then I come back in and write another sentence. Then I have tea and turn the new sentence around. Then I read the two sentences over and turn them both around. Then I lie down on my sofa and I think. Then I get up and throw them out and start from the beginning. And if I knock off from this routine for as long as a day, I'm frantic with boredom and a sense of waste . . ."

The intimacy here is not in the literal application of Lonoff's words, but in what they mean—that writing is an intense, lonely, often frustrating exercise, that sometimes it can take hours to produce one simple sentence (remember the words of Joseph Conrad when he said that he could take an entire morning to insert a single adjective . . . and take the entire afternoon to remove it). These are the intimate details of a writer's life and craft, and readers like to hear about them. Most writers, myself included, need not look far to find an audience eager to hear about how we *write!* As if there's a mystical dimension we inhabit. So when Philip Roth describes the way his character, Lonoff, writes, readers are bound to be interested, and when Roth details the writing agony with great detail, as he has done, the reader's interest rises accordingly.

Roth isn't *telling* us how Lonoff writes, he's *showing* us by having Lonoff do the talking and by having Lonoff describe it in a frame which is made up of obsession, perfection and creativity. Lonoff comes alive on the page, and the reader yearns for more.

That's what drama can do.

14

Be Specific

There's a writer's adage that goes like this . . . *when writing about war, write about one man's war; when writing about peace, write about one man's war.*

Think about it. How do we personalize a story so it gets under the reader's skin? How do we touch the reader's sensitivities? We do it by allowing the reader to *feel* what's happening; we excite interest.

A lot of ways to do this, of course, but one approach, certainly, is to provide the reader with solid information so he or she will grow comfortable with what we want them to identify with. The more they come to know, the greater the chances they'll identify, and that's when we get our sympathetic reader.

And that's when readers write us complimentary letters.

The more they come to know . . . it's a reasonable goal because all of us have trouble feeling deeply for people or places we hardly know. If we want readers to empathize, we must be willing to give them enough so they *can* empathize. Generalities don't do it, specifics do.

When writing about war, write about one man's war . . . there's nothing magic in this, but when we weave a story, we're not going to get far unless we have interesting characters. A war story without interesting characters isn't going to be much of a story, and the reader isn't going to feel much. War in the abstract doesn't carry the impact that war in the foxhole does.

> God, how he hated writing home. Trying not to let them see how scared he really was, how the nightly mortar barrage caused his toes to curl so he'd have cramps through his thighs for hours, and he'd be forced to crawl to the latrine . . .

That's being specific, and we can feel for the young soldier in the depths of his fear.

> Their time on the line brought nightly mortar attacks, but casualties were light and there was no thought of bringing up reinforcements. The fighting was sporadic . . .

That's being general, and while the same topic is covered, the writing, itself, is not personalized. What's happened is that in one instance we've used a close-up camera, while in the other we've gone to a wide-angle lens. When we're talking about dramatic effect, it's obvious which one has the greater impact. With the close-up we get to see the dimples and the warts and the worry lines . . . with the wide angle lens, we get broad perspectives and shadows but not touchable imagery.

One shows, the other tells.

When writing about peace, write about one man's war . . . here again we have the choice between general and specific, but now we've added another element: in the midst of war, can one man find peace? Peace and war, contending. It's an obvious tension-maker (we explored how tension is a dramatic, show-don't-tell device in Chapter Three), and for that we have built-in drama: the conflict between war and peace on the same stage. Instead of writing about how one frightened soldier tries to do his military duty, we'd write about another soldier's refusal to continue and why. We'd personalize it, too, and the reader would come to know the character. There would be drama and identification, and a tight close-up.

Specifics do make things more dramatic, but that doesn't mean *any* zero-in will do or that we need not worry about being *too* specific. Familiar writing rules apply here, as well, and we must match our technique with the purpose we want it to serve. Would it be necessary, for example, to spend a page and a half describing a room scene, when the room will play only a peripheral role in the story's outcome? Does dramatic effect require us to portray a character's most minor warts and blemishes when these will have little influence on why the character acts or speaks in a certain way? Specifics mean *relevant* specifics, enough to garner the reader's interest but not too much to kill it.

A careful writer understands this well. Take a look at the way Louise Erdrich, in her novel, *Tracks,* handles the description of a small town in North Dakota to which a young native-American woman flees after she has been driven off the reservation because some believe her possessed of evil spirits.

When she got to Argus in the year 1913 it was just a grid of six streets on either side of the railroad depot. There were two elevators, one central, the other a few miles west. Two stores competed for the trade of the three hundred citizens, and three churches quarreled with one another for their souls. There was a frame building for Lutherans, a heavy brick one for Episcopalians, and a long narrow shingle Catholic church. This last had a slender steeple twice as high as any building or tree.

This is as far as she goes in describing the town, yet a relevant portion of the story will take place here. She gives us a close-up of several items—the churches, the grain elevators, the railroad depot, two stores. We understand the size of the town because there's a gridwork of six streets on either side of the depot, and only three hundred people live here.

She doesn't tell us the design of the railroad depot nor does she describe the width of the streets or the colors of the buildings. What she does is to concentrate on the churches, and through this we gain a vivid picture of the town.

There are more churches than stores, and there are only three hundred humans to fill up these churches. That's a lot of church space for a town this size. More churches than stores . . . three hundred people for three churches . . . these are the kind of specifics that grab a reader's attention and develop a sense of drama. They offer an unusual symmetry, and a reader has to imagine it in order to understand it.

But that's not all. Take a careful look at the way she portrays the churches: they "quarreled" with one another. Note how she personalizes their effect, how she turns them into images. Now we know they don't get along well, especially when it comes to reaching for the souls of the town's three hundred. The churches "quarreled" for these souls. Can't we identify with that?

There's more. See how she describes each of the churches. The Lutherans had a frame building, the Episcopalians a heavy brick structure, the Catholics a shingled place with a high steeple. Not only is she providing us a close-up, but she's also contrasting the way each of these houses of worship was built. Out of this contrast we catch the individuality of each religion, and we come to know them better. The contrast, itself, gives this to us, and the result is a clearer portrayal because each is seen in perspective against the others. Contrast, in the realm of the specific, makes the image more vivid. See how it works:

- to portray an emotion (cruelty, for example) develop its opposite (gentleness)
- to depict a character, produce contrasting traits (greedy at work, generous at home)
- to offer comedy, contrast exaggeration with reality (a naive bumbler in charge of a mid-city bus which careens wildly)

Keep things specific, and what do we have? Imagery which becomes drama which becomes showing.

We've said it before, but it bears repeating: For drama to work the reader has to *feel* something, it must affect him or her in some emotional way. Otherwise, it's but an exercise in putting words on a page with no images and little impression. To be dramatic we have to show what happens, and this means we have to think creatively and reach for those tools which can make our task easier.

One of these tools is to make an appeal to the senses, and while this is covered more fully in Chapter Seventeen, sense appeal has application with writing specifically, too. As we develop our specifics, building an appeal to the senses aids in creating dramatic effect. For example, if we wish to portray beauty, we could detail those things which affect what we see or taste or smell . . .

> The colors on the horizon were purples and golds with but a hint of sparkling blue, and I could smell the honey scent of jacaranda which seemed to lie on my tongue as the sweetest blossom . . .

The more specific we grow with our appeal to the senses, the more the portrayal takes shape (though, here again, we don't want to overdo it; think relevance and purpose), and the more the shape appears the more dramatic we have become. Sense appeal doesn't work when we stay general. Let's try the selection above and see what happens:

> The colors on the horizon were lovely, and it made me feel happy and content. What I smelled and tasted were fine, too . . .

No showing here, only telling. The senses aren't activated, and there's little excitement. But get specific, and then the reader gets involved.

Take a look at the way Henry David Thoreau described the passage of time in his nineteenth-century idyll along the shores of Walden Pond:

> "Sometimes, in a summer morning, having taken my accustomed bath, I sat in my sunny doorway from sunrise til noon, rapt in a revery, amidst pines and hickories and sumachs while the birds sang around or flitted noiseless through the house, until by the sun falling in at my west window, or the noise of some traveler's wagon on the distant highway, I was reminded of the lapse of time . . ."

Note how specific he becomes, how he mentions his bath and sitting in his sunny doorway (which brings pleasure to his sense of touch), the sun falling in at the west window (which shows us what he sees), the birds singing and the traveler's wagon on the distant highway (which perks up his sense of hearing) and the pines and hickories and sumachs (which imply his sense of smell). All of this in one short paragraph, yet it certainly doesn't overwhelm us. We find ourselves feeling these things along with Thoreau, and as his tranquility develops, we, too, experience a gentle peace.

But he could have written this in more general terms, without an appeal to the senses. His point was to show how tranquil he could become by allowing nature to wash over him, and he could have told us:

"Sometimes during the summer I'd take a bath and sit in the sun, thinking. All morning long I'd do this, letting nature give me pleasure . . .

We can't get much of a mental picture from this because the words don't *show* what he was feeling (except for pleasure). The sentences aren't specific enough to generate an appeal to our senses, they succeed only in providing us with information, not drama, and our involvement drops.

There's one other thing to note in Thoreau's passage . . . the fact he *implies* an appeal to his senses with the pines and hickories and sumachs (he doesn't actually state he smells them) doesn't lessen their impact. The important thing is that the appeal to the senses exists, and it is equally as vivid this way, even if it is implied. It isn't necessary to write: "I blinked at the blue trumpet blossoms from the jacaranda . . ." We can put it: "A tiny droplet of water sparkled at the edge of the blue trumpet jacaranda blossom . . ." Readers will understand that to write this way we had to have been examining the flower. We imply we're looking at it, and that's enough. The key, above all else, is to be specific.

Not all specifics, of course, will create drama; there must be a connection between the subject and the emotions we wish to stir in the reader. A treatise on developing a sanitary landfill might get extremely specific, but I'm not sure it would carry much drama (unless it was the setting for a murder or the report, itself, became the source of conflict in the story which followed). Without more, this type of specific detail is telling rather than showing, because the emotion we wish to stir is intellectual curiosity, not anger or greed or sympathy, or envy— no emotion at all. How can a reader find anything to identify with here?

But let's make the subject more exciting: a car chase, backstage at a television show, a nighttime stroll through a cemetery. Here, now, we have the foundation for creating emotion, and a connection between subject and emotion can be made. A car chase—*fear, revenge;* backstage at a television show—*excitement, pride;* a nighttime stroll through a cemetery—*bravado, nervousness.*

The next step should be obvious—we describe the emotion specifically in order to draw in the reader. Fear, for example:

My heart beat wildly as we roared along ridge road, I could scarcely catch my breath and my mind was spinning aimlessly . . .

That's showing.

One thing readers always seem to enjoy is prose with the most current flavor; that is, prose which goes into events and circumstances—even dialogue—on the cutting edge of what we know or want to know. Taken to its extreme, this is what science fiction is all about—stories which deal with things we wish we did know about. But short of this, stories that are happening *now* have an appeal because if the writer is doing his or her work well, and we can imagine the events taking place at our fingertips . . .

We'll wish we could jump into the scene.

Current happenings have built-in allure for a writer because the reader doesn't have to imagine a different time period, and if the characters are familiar, the reader doesn't have to imagine people he or she might not understand. In effect, the writer has a head start in creating the scene, and what's left is to make it dramatic enough so the reader can truly jump in.

Getting specific is one sure way of causing it to happen. The formula is quite simple: take one subject on the cusp of current events, add a relevant emotional connection and stir in enough specifics to keep a high level of interest. The result will be a dramatic scene.

   The current event . . . a terrorist attack

   The emotional connection . . . fear and revenge

   The specifics . . . step-by-step happening

There's no way to avoid showing this scene instead of telling it. The drama is too acute and the excitement too sustained.

Let's take another example. In the novel, *Day of the Cheetah,* by Dale Brown, we have a story of a Russian plan to hijack the United States's newest, most advanced fighter plane, called "Dreamstar." Early in the book, Dreamstar and its older rival, "Cheetah," are side by side on the runway waiting to take off and fight a mock duel in the sky. J.C. is the pilot of Cheetah and Patrick is his navigator. James is flying Dreamstar solo. Both planes are in radio contact with the tower and with one another:

   "Pre-take-off and line-up checks," Patrick said over interphone.

   "Roger," J.C. replied. "In progress."

   "Storm two ready for release," James suddenly radioed in.

   "Amazing," Patrick said to J.C. "He's already done with a pre-take-off checklist twice as complicated as ours." He keyed the UHF radio switch. "Standby, Storm two."

   "Roger."

   "MAW switch set to V-sub-X max performance take-off." J.C. read off the most critical switch positions for the mission-adaptive-wing mode, and Patrick saw that the leading and trailing edges of wings had curved into a long, deep high-lift airfoil.

   "Canard control and engine nozzle control switches set to 'AUTO ALPHA'," J.C. continued. "This will be a constant alpha take-off . . ."

There's nothing more current than the exotic portrayal of the most advanced weapon systems in our armed forces, and this is what we have here. Though Dreamstar and Cheetah are figments of the author's imagination, undoubtedly, the line between fiction and fact might be chillingly close. Yet we have to start from the premise that this is a novel and that the author disclaims any special depiction of actual weapons systems. Even so, we aren't far off the real thing, and here's where the drama comes in. It's exciting to be close enough to a sophisticated fighter plane to learn what the pilots might say to one another, and in spite of one voice saying *it's only a novel,* another voice is also saying, *this could actually be true, the author knows what he is talking about.*

Some have called a book like this a techno-novel, for there are many instances of words and phrases that speak to the afficiondo. But that doesn't mean the book lacks drama or excitement or any of the other elements that make a good story; all it means is that part of the book's allure lies in its wide use of technical jargon, which, in turn, carries its own appeal.

This techno-speak turns the story into showing, showing, showing; it develops drama. First, by its nature, techno-speak rides the crest of current military awareness, and as we've seen, this is, in itself, exciting and dramatic. Readers like to read about what's hot and new and unusual. Second, see how specific the characters get with their dialogue and actions—"Maw switch" . . . "V-sub-X max performance" . . . "mission-adaptive-wing mode" . . . "high-lift airfoil" . . . "Canard control" . . . "engine nozzle control switches" . . . "AUTO ALPHA" . . . "alpha take-off" . . . These are techno-words and phrases, and I can't imagine the majority of readers could understand them. I know I don't.

But does it really matter? Do we have to know exactly what's happening to the planes as they prepare to take off? Probably not because the real story will occur once they do take off and attempt to outduel one another in the sky. These techno-words and phrases add atmosphere, to be sure, and because they sound so "official" and relevant, they add zest to the story.

They show us what an exotic fighter plane and its weapons systems must do before they head into the sky. And because the subject is enticing enough and because the emotional connection deals with competition and rivalry, the more specific we become, the more dramatic the story will be.

The formula works, it really does.

15

"Now Suppose . . ."

A few years ago my late wife and I wrote a book for writers on the mechanics and development of plotting. The point we made was that no one has a monopoly on story ideas or story plots, that they are there for the taking. We devised thirteen "plot motivators" which we felt would serve any conceivable story purpose. Vengeance and catastrophe and love and hate and rebellion and rivalry and ambition—we called them plot motivators because they *ignited* a story, they *motivated* what would happen.

We got the idea for the book from a New England writer's conference where we listened to a novelist describe how he came up with *his* idea for *his* book. "My plot is based on an ancient Greek legend," he told us, "on the obsessive desire of Apollo for Daphne, after he has seen her bathing in a clear mountain stream. But Zeus intervenes and neutralizes Apollo's ardor."

The novelist went on to show how this series of events became the focus for his own work. "Now suppose the setting could be changed to the New Hampshire woods," he suggested, "and suppose Daphne is a nubile college girl, and suppose Apollo turns out to be a virile, frustrated local man . . ." and he went on to draw a close parallel between his novel and the Greek legend from which it derived.

"As you can see, I found a plot," the novelist exclaimed, and we wrote:

> "Indeed he did! By elementary changes in time, setting, cultural background he was able to map strategy and attitudes to bring everything into a contemporary frame."

Though our book concerned techniques of plotting, we realized that creating one plot from another often spurred the use of "now suppose . . ." or "what if . . ." because each story would have a mind of its own and require an innovative twist from the story that gave it life. It was all right to steal a plot, but that was only the first step; now the more intimate details of the story line had to be worked on, and here we were left to our own creative devices. "Now suppose . . ." and "what if . . ." became the spark.

Following our New England novelist and his story a bit further, we wrote:

> "The audience's creative wheels start spinning, What if . . . this plot were set in wartime? What if . . . the woman were a journalist and the protagonist a villager in a repressive South American country? What if . . . he intrigues her after frightening her and they become friends . . . then lovers? What happens to her old boy friend . . . his old girl friend?"

This push to the imagination is the way many stories have developed, and we can apply it in even the most elementary of circumstances: boy meets girl, boy loses girl, boy and girl are reunited. Let's try "now suppose . . ."

boy meets girl: (now suppose boy and girl are rivals for a particular prize)

boy loses girl: (now suppose girl wins prize and boy sulks)

boy and girl are reunited: (now suppose boy realizes girl will do more with the prize than he would)

The point to "now suppose . . ." is to generate the wheels of the imagination so that a series of word-pictures can result. When we challenge ourselves . . . "now suppose . . ." we are really forcing our minds to come up with ideas and solutions that will add vibrancy and depth to our story line. We are seeking to expand the story horizon and dramatize what will happen next.

Let's look at a familiar story and see where it takes us: in Shakespeare's *Julius Caesar* we have Cassius convincing Brutus that Caesar must be assassinated because of his over-arching ambition. At this point the circumstances of the story are easily transferable to a modern-day plot (a conspiracy to bring down a powerful leader because his surge for power threatens the conspirators and their plans). Brutus, Cassius and the others carry out their plans to attack Caesar, *only they fail!* Caesar survives. Now suppose what happens . . .

- Caesar institutes a reign of terror, seeking vengeance
- Caesar resigns because he fears for his life (not so likely, but, then, we can make *our* Caesar anything we wish him to be)
- Caesar shows forgiveness and throttles back his ambition, even offering to share power with Mark Antony

Or let's inject "now suppose . . ." even earlier in the story. As Cassius tries to recruit Brutus, now suppose:

- Brutus *pretends* to go along, but his loyalty remains with Caesar and he reports what is happening

- Brutus sees this as a chance to feed his own ambition, and he demands to be installed in Caesar's place
- Brutus is really in love with Calphurnia, Caesar's wife, and sees he can get rid of his rival and have her, too

As we develop these alternative plot lines, notice what is happening . . . our imaginations are working to set up word-pictures that will spur a new story direction. But we aren't thinking in linear terms—that is, in narrative prose lines on a page of paper. We're thinking in three-dimensional creative steps, in portrayals and events as they occur before us! For example, initially, we don't see Brutus's pretense to Cassius as simple words:

Ah, but let him think me in when I know to be out, let him relate to me so I can relate to him, let him foul his cry so even the hawks shall hide . . .

Instead, we conjure a portrait of Brutus offering a concerned, though unemotional, facade as Cassius tries to recruit him; then we see Cassius earnestly pleading his case; then we imagine where they are speaking, perhaps a plaza or an outdoor market; then we have a sense that there are others milling about; then we hear voices, Cassius with a hint of sharpness, Brutus more stolid, more uncommitted . . .

And, finally, after we've completed the portrait—in our minds, of course—we sit down to write the words. This is the essence of creativity, and this is how we take an old story and make something new from it. Every time we use "now suppose . . ." we force ourselves to show, instead of tell.

Put another way, "An idea is a flame that ignites the individual creative imagination . . ." writes novelist William Tapply. "An idea sets off a complicated chain reaction, a sequence of imagined events that the writer transfers into scenes populated by imaginary people. That is a story." Sparking our imagination is the key, and it's accomplished by pushing ourselves to new paths.

Tapply goes on: "Learning to ask those 'what if' and 'then what' and 'what next' questions; to experiment by linking two or more apparently unrelated premises; to follow my imagination as it wonders and supposes; to know when it is leading somewhere and to shut it off when it's not—that's what's necessary . . ."

And he adds something we'd all agree with: "*It's not easy.*" Yet, as writers, we must rely upon our imaginations, and what we must learn to do is to direct our imaginations into productive paths so we develop a cohesive story instead of a jumbled, miscellaneous mass of ideas. Using "Now suppose . . ." or "What if . . ." is a technique for doing exactly that. It provides us discipline and a measuring rod for our creativity.

Let's follow one of William Tapply's suggestions: the link of two apparently unrelated premises. Imagine two completely dissimilar individuals, settings and storylines and see if they can be woven together. A religious icon in a Himalayan monastery with a coarse, violence-prone urban biker, for example; or an Australian shark hunter and a group of homeless Iraqi children. The more dissimilar the better. Then we say, "Now suppose . . ."

And our story takes off.

This is the way it might have worked with Russell Banks and his book, *Continental Drift*, a story that begins in New Hampshire and ends off the coast of Florida. There are two dissimilar themes running through this book, yet one knows (because Banks tells us in the first few pages) that the storylines will converge, and, in fact, they do. It's a story about Bob Dubois, an oil burner repairman, who wants to leave the cold Northeast and find something new in Florida. He yearns for more excitement and a less arduous life.

Simultaneously, the book relates the odyssey of Vonise, a young Haitian woman, and her son and a few others who flee Haiti for the promised land of America. Their trip is long and terrifying, as they island hop across the Caribbean in leaky trawlers, open boats and on foot.

Here, now, we have two dissimilar people: a white, blue collar New Englander and a Black, uneducated Haitian woman; two dissimilar storylines: a man who is tired of a routine job and a routine life, and a woman who runs to save her life and that of her son; two dissimilar settings: benign, good-life Florida and terror-filled Haiti and assorted scary interludes at sea and in the islands.

Finally, the worlds of Bob Dubois and Vonise meet with calamitous results. Bob has become a small-boat captain, and he convinces himself he needs money. So he agrees to smuggle Haitians, including Vonise, into America. He goes to New Providence in the Bahamas to pick them up, and here's the way the author describes the initial meeting between Bob and the Haitians (this is on page 302, fully two-thirds into the novel):

> They seem so fragile to Bob, so delicate and sensitive, that he's suddenly frightened for them. Even the young men, with their hair cut close to the skull seem fragile. He wants to reassure them somehow to say that nothing will hurt them as long as they are under his care, nothing, not man or beast or act of God. But he knows he can't even tell them where they are going, what time it is, what his name is. Not with the half-dozen words and phrases of Québecois he learned by accident as a child . . .

At the outset of this book it seemed incomprehensible that two such dissimilar characters could find common ground. Yet it's a tribute to the author that he kept the

story going and slowly, carefully brought them together. If we retraced his steps, we'd see he asked himself the questions William Tapply suggested:
- "Now suppose . . ." or "What if . . . ?"
- "Then what . . . ?"
- "What next . . . ?"

Each time the story responded to these questions an element of drama was injected because a new storyline was developed. As with any new storyline, the opportunity to show, rather than tell, was there, and Russell Banks took advantage, using techniques that we're familiar with.

The real value in working with dissimilar storylines and dissimilar characters is the demands it places upon us and our creative imaginations. We *must* come up with intriguing story development in order to work the dissimilar portions closer and closer together. A simple chronological story, for example, wouldn't put these demands upon us because we know that the events and circumstances have a linear certainty; time controls how the story will proceed, and while the demand for drama is every bit as strong, we don't have to face the added burden of coping with a dissimilar storyline.

Using "Now suppose . . ." isn't limited to tying dissimilar storylines (and/or dissimilar characters and settings) together, it works in other places, too. If we think of it as a *tool* for prodding our creative imaginations and for getting us to places we might never have expected to be, then we can understand its value as a drama producer. Because it *forces* us to think in word-pictures since we're asking ourselves where the story should move next. When we ask ourselves, "Now suppose . . . ," we don't imagine words on the page—at least not at first. We conjure word-pictures, which then become words on the page when we apply them.

And "Now suppose . . ." had a broad reach. For example, if we take a disagreeable character who has led a disagreeable life and place him in disagreeable circumstances, the challenge to turn all of that into a sympathetic portrait is daunting. "Now suppose . . ." we ask ourselves, "this character says or feels or does things which neutralize all the disagreeable aspects of his story. Is it possible to do?"

William Kennedy was able to do it with his novel, *Ironweed*, the story of Francis Phelan, in the early 1930s, who has been living the life of a bum ever since he killed a strike breaker during labor unrest a dozen years before and fled his hometown of Albany, New York. Francis has been living in hobo camps, doorways and the occasional flophouse; he has had no permanent job and no permanent address. He wears cast-off clothing and rarely bathes.

Now he has returned to Albany and his memory conjures the traumatic time when he was holding his baby son and dropped him on his head and killed him. It pushed him out of his marriage and onto the streets, where he eventually killed the strike breaker.

Here, then, is a portrait of a murdering, cowardly, smelly old man whose life is a shambles, most of it brought on by his own failings. It's the rare reader who could find much to like in such a character *unless* the writer is able to turn things around with uncommon deftness. Watch how William Kennedy does it in a graveyard scene where Francis has come to commune at the grave of his dead baby son:

> Francis found the grave without a search. He stood over it and reconstructed the moment when the child was slipping through his fingers into death. He prayed for a repeal of time so that he might hang himself in the coal bin before picking up the child to change his diaper. Denied that, he prayed for his son's eternal

peace in the grave. It was true the boy had not suffered at all in his short life, and he had died too
quickly of a cracked neckbone to have felt pain: a
sudden twist and it was over. *Gerald Michael Phelan*,
his gravestone said, *born April 13, 1916, died April
26, 1916. Born on the 13th, lived 13 days. An un-
lucky child who was much loved.*

Tears oozed from Francis's eyes . . .

By the time this passage is finished, even the most hard-
ened reader will feel the first stirrings of sympathy for
Francis, and the reason is that the author gives Francis a
human dimension (grief and remorse) to which all of us
can relate. Is there anything more devastating than the
death of an innocent child? Is there anything more shattering than realizing personal responsibility for that death? As
we enmesh ourselves in Francis's sadness, we quickly
wipe away the unattractive images of the way he lives and
looks. Now it's *poor Francis!* . . . not, Francis Phelan,
that bum!

And William Kennedy has accomplished this because he
challenged himself to resurrect a highly tarnished portrait.
"Now suppose . . . this disagreeable man could be made
attractive . . ." That's what he set out to do, and in a few
short lines he accomplished it. For us, the bottom line is
he injected drama into his story, he added excitement and
interest.

Now suppose . . . "Francis Phelan remembers his dead
son and rekindles his guilt and his grief at the baby's
graveside . . ." This moves the story along and provides a
sympathetic characterization.

Kennedy is *showing* us how it happens.

Remember *Lord of the Flies*, that classic by William
Golding about young boys stranded on a tropic island
after the outbreak of nuclear war and how they develop
their own society? As a work of fiction it was also a look at

the value underpinnings of British society because the boys, as proper young British lads, mirrored the class consciousness and the political pluralism of their parents. To many it was an uncomfortable portrait because it showed less adherence to democracy and more towards authoritarianism.

Now comes Marianne Wiggins, and she asks herself "Is this the way the girls would do it?" She means if a bunch of young women endured a similar fate, would they have handled it the same way? So she wrote *John Dollar,* a novel about eight young English school girls and their school mistress who become marooned on an island in the South China Sea during a sailing expedition out of Rangoon, Burma. "Now suppose . . ." the girls had to survive on this uninhabited island, how would they do it?"

What Marianne Wiggins did was to take a familiar plot and add her own twist to it. It would be girls, not boys, and they would act *differently*. But they still would have to survive. Can't we imagine Marianne Wiggins asking those "Now suppose . . ." questions? Or the "Then what . . ." and "What next . . ." questions? How would the girls organize themselves, how would they deal with food collecting, how would they handle the relationship with their school mistress/chaperone who is now as vulnerable as they are?

How would they cope? Here's an example (Nolly and Amanda are two of the girls):

Nolly walks down to the surf, responding to the call of nature, in accordance to Law Number Eleven. Amanda's mother was compulsive about conditions, everybody knew—she was particularly opposed to Touching Things, ever since Amanda's father took up with his Burmese. Amanda's mother acted as if only strict *conditions* in the household could prevent them all from catching something awful and she'd become a one woman army against contagion. Amanda had inherited her mother's skills—

Law Number Ten. No one is allowed to peepee anywhere but in the ocean

Law Number Eleven. No one is allowed to pong above low tide

Law Number Twelve. Everyone will keep her knickers (a) clean (b) dry . . .

This obviously isn't the way the boys in *Lord of the Flies* set about doing things, but these are young girls we're dealing with, and the author understands their differing sensibilities. The point is to see that "Now suppose . . ." is the springboard for an entire story, and that once begun, the story can keep going by the occasional prod of "What next . . ." and "Then what . . ." The drama inherent in a story of survival like this is clear—these are innocent girls caught in a harsh environment, and they have nothing but their training and their grit to fall back upon. It doesn't take much for a reader to feel empathy, but even this would dissipate if the story faltered. Once the image of these girls, fearful but determined, becomes blurred, the .drama falls away and the word-pictures dissolve.

So it was important for the author to remind herself to "Now suppose . . . ," and this she certainly did. There was anger and fear and love and redemption along the way, and each time the storyline jumped ahead, the word-pictures would form. By asking herself to "Now suppose . . ." Marianne Wiggins created scenes which showed us how it was on that cruel little island . . .

And we were able to see it.

16

Focus That Point of View

The winch handle hadn't been used in years. It was rust-crusted and brittle, and Sam wondered if it would break apart as he turned it. He had no choice, of course. The only way they'd get across the ravine was by winching the foot bridge into position. "Not going to be easy," he murmured.

Bobby glanced at the sharp blue sky and scudding clouds, but his mind was on his stomach. Nothing since he and Sam had shared the lake trout at breakfast. He didn't feel like moving any farther. "I'm tired," he said, flopping down on an outcropping.

"Must be two hundreds yards across," Sam figured, staring down at the sheer rock that plummeted to the green-canopied forest below.

Bobby remembered today was Tuesday and tonight was his favorite television time. He thought of the red-faced policeman whose inept attempts at law enforcement made him laugh. "I like television when it's funny," he said . . .

As we work on beefing our writing skills, inevitably we'll come face to face with that disarmingly simple concept, *point of view*. Through whose eyes is the story to be shown (or, as the late editor William Sloane asked, through whose *means of perception* is the story shown?), are there different *types* of point of view, when should we change point of view? Questions like these are at the root of the concept, and every writer has to weigh them as he or she produces the story. Quite simply, point of view is crucial for any dramatic showing, and its improper use can force a story out of a groove.

The general idea of point of view is simple; it's in the application that confusion threatens. Basically, point of view is the lens through which a scene or an event or a reaction is seen and/or experienced. It can be personal and subjective ("I could feel traces of the searing heat through my rubberized suit . . ."), and the story must then be limited to what "I" see or hear or grasp. It can be personal and objective ("He could feel traces of the searing heat through his rubberized suit . . ."), and the story remains limited to what that character sees, hears or grasps. It can be omniscient and objective ("They all could feel traces of the searing heat through their rubberized suits . . ."), and there are no limits on what can be seen, heard or grasped. The story is seen through a lens that towers over the characters instead of a lens that is imbedded within them, and the author is able to move things around at will.

In the opening selection, note how the point of view shifts from paragraph to paragraph. First we have Sam's viewpoint, then we have Bobby's, then Sam's, then Bobby's. Nothing wrong with this, of course, *providing* they are focusing on the same thing. It's a common technique to shift point of view within a scene, when we wish to generate excitement and tension. Bang! Bang! Bang!

. . . first one viewpoint, then another, back and forth quickly, quickly, quickly . . .

There's drama in all of this. But when the focus is dispersed, when the differing viewpoints are spotlighting different things, then the drama begins to fade . . . as in the opening selection. Follow the action line:

> *1st paragraph:* Sam is concerned about winching up the bridge
>
> *2nd paragraph:* Bobby is hungry
>
> *3rd paragraph:* Sam sees the ravine as wide and dangerous
>
> *4th paragraph:* Bobby thinks about television

There's no focus here, and the result is that the reader is jerked back and forth without a sense of continuity. The drama lapses and along with it the reader's attention. If we wanted to tie all the events together—the bridge, Bobby's hunger, the ravine and Bobby's television watching—we'd have to end up telling instead of showing because circumstances had become so spread out. We'd have to narrate the connections, and we'd have to explain how these differing items could all be tied together.

That's the problem with a lack of focus—it forces us away from the drama and into exposition in order to make sure the reader isn't confused. It's like the long distance runner who is more comfortable examining the people lined along the race course than concentrating on where the race is going and how far it will be to the finish line. When the runner realizes he's dropping farther and farther behind, he knows he has to rush to catch up, and this will cause a change in his rhythm and his style. He can't expect to regain focus right away, either. Focusing takes time and energy, and he has to work back up to it.

And just like the runner who rushes to catch the field, the writer who doesn't focus well will have a large gap in the drama to make up. Trying to fill it unnaturally will have the same effect on style and rhythm as rushing did on the runner—herky-jerkiness and a ragged ending.

Now, if we wanted to focus properly on Sam and Bobby we'd have them *both* dealing with the problems of the bridge and the ravine (instead of diverting the reader with Bobby's hunger and television watching). Shifting the point of view between them is no problem and, in fact, can add to the drama of the scene, especially since there will be some tension and uncertainty until they get over the ravine. The quick shifts in viewpoint add excitement and provide the reader an opportunity to involve himself or herself. Both characters are focused on the same challenge, and the viewpoint shift serves to enlarge the way the challenge can be felt and understood.

That's showing, that's drama.

Obviously, the safest way to avoid the problems of shifting point of view is to maintain the story through the eyes of a single character. The point of view remains constant, and the attitudes or reactions of others don't get in the way. Yet it isn't quite that simple. Even with a steady, single point of view, focus can wax and wane. For example . . .

He wondered whether Mary really intended to go through with it. He could usually read her facial expressions, and the determination that marked her decision-making simply wasn't there this time. But talk of decision making! There had been Harriet—his *special* Harriet—who had shared his life after college and who hated to decide anything. "What'll we have for dinner?" he'd ask. "What do *you* want?" she'd answer. "Where'll we go tonight?" he'd ask. "Where would *you* like to go?" she'd answer. He remembered the time she inherited some money . . .

Here's a single viewpoint with a shifting focus. We start out with Mary and we end up with Harriet, and the questions about Mary are momentarily forgotten as the narrator rushes to describe a Harriet anecdote. But note the first two sentences. They seem to be saying that Mary is an important character in this scene, if not in the story. Should concern about her be pushed away like this? There's a place for the Harriet anecdote, of course, but it shouldn't come at the expense of Mary's characterization. The question of Mary's decision making is left hanging, and the result is an incomplete image when Harriet comes on the scene. If mention of Mary's decision making was important for the story, the focus should be there for awhile, and the drama can then bloom. But as it stands the drama is cut short because the focus has shifted, and when it's time to pick up the threads of Mary's decision making, it may become necessary to do some explaining in order to catch up with the story.

That means telling, not showing.

Take a look at the way John Updike handles the single, focused point of view in his novel, *Roger's Version*. Roger, the narrator, is a Methodist minister who teaches in divinity school. Dale, a young man who is involved with Roger's niece, comes to see him seeking help for a grant to study the existence of God. Dale enters the story on the first page and their discussion (which covers religion, history, existence of God and how Roger teaches religious theory) goes on for 27 pages, all of it seen through Roger's eyes. Near the end of their discussion, Roger says:

". . . But I really must go to my class Mr. Kohler. I *will* say . . .

He jumped at the gap, the glimmer of light. "Yessir?"

"I probably shouldn't say anything," I allowed, and

wondered, indeed, why I was seeking collusion, adopting a toadying, seductive tone with this pale and presuming young man, "but it *would* be a relief, as far as I am concerned, to underwrite something around here other than black or feminist studies. On these pathetic papers on 'street religion,' which amounts to gypsy fortune telling and superstitions about numbers on license plates and subway cars. If you do go ahead with the application, you can say on it you talked with me and I found your ideas and facts . . . what shall we say—?"

"Compelling?"

"Amusing."

Throughout the 27 pages of this conversation Updike does not enter Dale's head, and we never deviate from Roger's point of view. But the focus is more than from a single viewpoint, it's also on a single subject. Roger measures Dale and weighs his ideas, he probes and picks at Dale's motivations and conclusions, and he lets us in on how he is thinking, so that by the end of the 27 pages we have come to know both characters intimately.

And that's why this becomes showing and not telling. We *feel* what these characters are feeling and we understand why they have come to their judgments. By allowing us, the readers, inside Roger's head and heart we experience what he experiences. And we don't need to be told what is going on. The drama is there before us, and the focus is clear and unambiguous.

But suppose we do want to shift the focus yet retain the same point of view? Suppose we want to have a character focusing on more than one object yet keep the drama from blurring? It can be done, and it has the obvious benefit of snapping the story back and forth between the different objects and of developing action, but . . . be careful! As we saw with Mary and Harriet, it's not difficult to go off on a tangent and become immersed with one of the objects and lose sight of the other one. Somehow the writer must keep control of the viewpoint and the focus, and this is best accomplished by treating each object gingerly, not leaning too heavily in any direction. With Mary and Harriet the lean was definitely in Harriet's direction, and so the focus went there, even though it was Mary's decision making that appeared to be key. The drama will usually follow the focus (providing the focus is not blurred) and Harriet became the beneficiary, *even though Mary was the important one!* The point of view remained constant, but the focus was off base, and this certainly would have affected the story.

Yet in the hands of an accomplished writer a shifting focus with a single point of view can develop strong dramatic effect. Take a look at the way novelist John Gregory Dunne handles it in *Dutch Shea, Jr.,* his story of a depressed, marginally successful lawyer who defends petty criminals and is obsessed with the recent death of his daughter. He is divorced and lives in semi-poverty and here he has nodded off to sleep:

More bad dreams.

A priest, a rabbi and David Suskind.

The subject was suicide.

"The thing is, David . . ." Rabbi Steven ("with a *v*, David") Lesher is talking. Rabbi Steven Lesher held his cigarette by its sides, between thumb and index finger as if it were a joint. ". . . the thing is, your suicide makes a commitment to taking his own life. Your suicide . . ." Rabbi Steven Lesher took two quick hits off his filter tip ". . . your *average* suicide, mind you, has a vocation . . ." Another hit. ". . . in the same way I had a vocation for the rabbinate and Lionel here . . ."

CUT TO: Father Lionel Gill, C.S.P.

"... had a vocation for the priesthood, isn't that
right, Lionel?"

Father Lionel Gill, C.S.P. vigorously shook his
head.

"I think that's absolute nonsense, Jewboy."

What!

He woke . . .

Throughout this book the point of view is that of the
lead character, Dutch Shea, Jr., yet here we have the focus
on the television screen, or at least what seems to be
showing on the screen. But it's all a dream, every line of
television dialogue, and what's really happened is that
Dutch Shea, Jr. has controlled the point of view throughout, *even though our attention has been focused on the
screen!* It's his dream and his reactions we are witnessing,
and what comes over the television screen is the product
of his own mind. So while the focus has shifted, the point
of view hasn't, and the drama remains intact. We still
identify with Dutch Shea, Jr. because we understand that
the television portrayal comes from his own head, that it
is *he himself* all the way.

The author could have botched it, however, if he had
had his character acting like a spectator before the television screen, if he had not involved Dutch Shea, Jr. in what
was going on before his eyes. If he had had him, for
instance, settle himself before the screen and offer no
reactions to the television portrayals. This would have
shifted focus *and* point of view, and the drama would
have suffered because there was no connection between
the shifts. One had little or no relevance to the other, and
they would have hung in the air like twin branches, never
touching.

Sometimes, instead of shifting the focus and maintain-
ing the point of view, we can change the point of view and
maintain the focus. It's not easy and it must be carefully

thought out, but it can be done. The purpose remains the same: to build the drama and show what happens instead of explaining that it happened. Changing the point of view from character to character has the obvious advantage of avoiding that "bogged down" feeling when we find ourselves stretched to keep a single character and his or her point of view interesting. Most of us have experienced it, I know, where our character grows lifeless because we feel limited by what he or she can do or say or experience. Shifting the point of view can change all that even while we maintain that character's focus. For example:

> . . . I spent the next fifteen minutes cleaning the sink and scrubbing away the remnants of cyanide dust. When they got around to testing the milk, I didn't want any connection with *this* kitchen . . .
>
> *Confidential to Homicide Division:* Mayor's Office wants results on the group poisoning last weekend. They're getting pressure from families of deceased, and pressure on Mayor means pressure on us. I've decided to form a task force . . .

The point of view shift is pretty clear, but note that the focus—the poisoning—remains the same. The tension and the drama remain high because the focus hasn't wandered, and it's intensified because we see the story from two different points of view. In the first paragraph it's the subjective, first person approach, and there's no doubt this viewpoint will weave its way through the story. In the second paragraph we go to the point of view of the police, and while it's still subjective (in the sense that the police only know what the author wants them to know) it's still a different perspective. The memorandum technique isn't the only one by which this could have been done, though it seems particularly appropriate because if the point of view changes, perhaps the *lens* through which the point of view operates should change too. But we could have dialogue and action in the second paragraph, too, so long as the focus remained on the poisoning.

This is similar to the way Erica Jong handled a steady focus and a shifting point of view in her novel, *Any Woman's Blues*. Her lead character, Leila Sand, is a successful artist who has an obsessive love for Dart, a much younger man, who treats her with cavalier scorn but provides her with unabashed physical joy. Throughout the book the point of view remains that of Leila, in the first person, but from time to time the author resurrects a character, Isadora Wing, from an earlier novel, *Fear of Flying*. Erica Jong uses Isadora Wing as an alternate, though limited, point of view for Leila Sand, and the result gives a boost to the drama. Here's an example where Leila is trying to forget Dart by seeing another man:

> At moments, I have the strong sense that all I have here is the Italian counterpart of Dart—another Don Giovanni but an authentic one! The Mediterranean Man, who does the role *right*. Wax to receive and marble to retain. Have I merely fallen for Don Juan again?
>
> (*Sane mind:* Are you asking me or telling me?)
> *Isadora: I'm with her!*
> *Leila: Who?*
> *Isadora: Your sane mind!*
> *Leila: Will you please shut up and let me enjoy this?*
>
> We stay in the lagoon, squeezing out the last drop of moonlight. Then he takes me back to my hotel . . .

The focus remains clear. It's Leila's search for a man who will treat her better. But we see her confusion and uncertainty from more than one point of view. Isadora is the realist (as is her sane mind), while Leila is the romantic, and by giving us several sides of the problem, Erica Jong has made it more vivid and identifiable. There's certainly drama in the struggle between Isadora and Leila, because tension is a never-failing, drama-raising technique, and when we see something in different ways, the portrayal grows and grows. Think how much less dramatic it would have been if Leila had simply followed her thought processes through interior monologue, instead of engaging in this give and take. The monologue might have become dramatic through imagery and anecdotes, but here we have a sure-fire drama builder by means of the tension between Leila and Isadora (and sane mind, too). What Erica Jong does is to show us Leila's struggle by means of a shifting point of view.

One that keeps its focus intact.

17

Appeal to the Senses

There's an exercise I do with young people in order to stimulate their image-building. All writers must think in word-pictures and must develop techniques to call up those word-pictures. "Without these tools," I say, "writers are little more than machines, only capable of producing what they are told to produce, never developing a creative voice."

Think in word-pictures, I emphasize, *don't be content with one-word explanations* . . .

"What does rain sound like when it hits the roof?" I ask.

"Rat-a-tat, rat-a-tat . . ." comes an answer.

"And when if falls in the garden?"

"Splat-splat-splat-splat . . ."

And when it falls on a pond?"

"Ping, ping, ping . . ."

"Do we feel differently, depending on the sound?"

Puzzled faces, furrowed brows. Different sounds create different images, I tell them, and it's up to the writer to develop these images into dramatic word-pictures. For example, if rain fell on a wooden roof, it would make a different sound than if it fell on a tin roof, and the writer has to be careful to fit the proper sound to the circumstances so the underlying emotions can surface. Rain on a tin roof—a machinegun like sound—would have a tendency to build tension because of its staccato beat and its harsh certainty. What kind of emotions would fit with this sound? Anger or confrontation or fear, even terror probably. But the one emotion that would not be in evidence would be mellowed complacency, and the reason is that the sounds of rain on the roof should stand for something in the story, otherwise, why bring them in at all?

And if we're feeling mellow, the rat-a-tat sounds of rain on the tin roof aren't appropriate. They neutralize the word-picture instead of enhance it.

The point is that what we hear can develop strong imagery because we associate the sounds in some way. Perhaps it's from our childhood, perhaps from a recent event, but what we hear *means* something to us, and it usually conjures a picture in our minds. For example, we hear the whistle of the wind during a rainstorm, and it might remind us of a similar event during our childhood, when we were trapped in a creaky old barn. Or perhaps we hear the sounds of a mellow guitar and it reminds us of a romantic time many years earlier. Or maybe it's a certain voice at a certain cadence that reminds us of a teacher or a co-worker . . .

And each time we're reminded, we develop the image of that person or that event, even if for only a moment. The emotions that are engendered by the sounds become part of the image and help to swell the picture. In the end, what we have is a dramatic portrayal based upon a sound or sounds that helped to create a word-picture. In short, we've *shown*, we've dramatized!

If this can happen to us as personal experience, then surely it can also happen to readers who devour our words on the written page. If we write about sounds in such a way as to create an image in the reader's mind, then we've planted that word-picture we so anxiously strive for, and the reader has a dramatic scene to enjoy. We've appealed to the reader's sense of hearing, and this has brought imagery and excitement where none existed before.

Hearing, or course, is not the only one of our senses where a word-picture can blossom. All of them, in fact— seeing, touching, tasting, smelling, as well as hearing— have the same capacity, and a writer who seeks to develop them will find a positive aid in story creation and drama build-up. An appeal to the senses has the advantage of involving the reader in fairly easy fashion because there's no mystery about where the reader stands—every reader has the same senses that we, the writer, have, and every reader's reaction will be pretty much the same as ours will be. If we write of something as "chocolaty, gooey, chewey . . . ," it wouldn't be hard to believe our own taste buds would be stimulated, and the same could be said for the reader. If we write of a "fog-shrouded night where vague shadows floated through the mist . . ." our sense of sight would cause us unease, and the same would happen to the reader who now imagines the scene.

As writers we need to understand that each time we wish to appeal to one of the reader's senses, we have to reckon with the circumstances that appeal will develop. For example, when I worked with the young people, what they heard from the same rainfall differed because of the surface the rain fell upon. The same approach must prevail with the other senses too: where the sound or the sight or the taste or the touch or the smell comes from will influence the word-picture that's created. Differing tastes will create differing word-pictures, just as differing touches will, or differing sights.

Some years ago, novelist Peggy Simpson Curry described how she stimulated her image-making ability by appealing to her own sense of smell. "Try, for example, recalling a series of odors," she wrote, "scents along riverbanks in early morning, in summer meadows, on the hills after rain, in certain clothing stores, on a downtown street at theatre time, in leather shops, bakery shops, candy stores, at a carnival, on your own block . . ." Each one of these might cause the reader to remember something which could stimulate an image in his or her mind, and if the nostalgia is strong enough, the writer might be able to develop it enough for an entire scene or a chapter. Let's see how it might work. Take the smells from the bakery shop . . .

- warm, yeasty
- pungent
- spicy

Don't these develop an image of a small store where good food is lined up, fresh and hot, doughy and browned? Can't we place ourselves right in the middle of this scene and experience the pleasure of the smells? Soon our other senses take over, and we picture the shop with its counter and shelves and row upon row of finely baked goods . . . and we feel the taste of this fresh, good food in our mouths . . . and we listen to the packaging of loaves of fresh bread or rolls in paper containers and we hear the cheerful banter between the customers and the bakery workers and the cash register ring as items are paid for . . .

All of this stimulated by the smells we remember from years past. But, of course, these smells from the bakery shop wouldn't be the same as the smells from the leather shop or from the odor of a summer meadow. Yet each, in its own way, stimulates us to think in images, and each contributes to our goal of showing instead of telling. We have to understand these differences while recognizing at the same time that they all contribute to the same goal.

Many writers don't carry the certainty that an appeal to *all* the senses is significant. They tend to concentrate on visual description only, ignoring anything about how a character's fictional world feels, tastes, smells or sounds. It's understandable, I suppose, because what we see is often the most substantial portion of what we come across. And if we write our story and don't touch on senses other than what is seen, we can do a credible job of producing readable prose.

> He watched the burley longshoreman limp to the gantry which was now locked in place for the night. He saw none of the work crew and realized the shift was over. The longshoreman took a pipe wrench from his overalls and peered up the dock before bending over one of the gantry wheels. The longshoreman was not aware he was being monitored . . .

See how more vivid it would be if we expanded our appeal to the senses:

> He could smell the receding tide as the burley longshoreman limped to the locked gantry and peered up the dock before taking a pipe wrench from his overalls. Soon darkness would cover the quiet of the pier and no one would know what happened. Everyone was gone now, and he could hear faint metallic grating as the longshoreman bent over one of the gantry wheels. He hoped the job would be finished before the tidal stench became too severe . . .

There's an appeal to hearing and smelling, as well as to seeing, in the second selection, and it gives us a more well-rounded word-picture. There are all sorts of things to hear and smell and see, even, perhaps, to touch on a shipyard pier in the early evening after the workers have gone home. If we follow the longshoreman by sight alone, we're limiting the atmosphere of our story. The smells and sounds can add to suspense or describe a disagreeable environment or provide a key to what was going on. They leaven the scene.

Take a look at the way novelist Lisa Alther does it in her book, *Bedrock*, the story of Clea, a successful travel photographer who has talked her husband into buying a home in Vermont and escaping from the city. She is tired of a career that has taken her all over the world, and she has decided she can live in Vermont and still do her photography. Here she contemplates some of the men who have passed through her life:

> She tried to picture some of her less crucial lovers but could summon only exotic foreign settings—a shaft of moonlight across a futon in a Japanese teahouse, a pink sand beach beneath clashing palms, a Paris pension with accordion music out of the window, a motel overlooking the sea in a small Australian beach town. She remembered baklava oozing honey in a Greek taverna and gray eyes gazing into hers on a train across the Nullarbor Plain . . .

Here we have a multiple appeal to the senses and the result is vivid and well rounded. Note the senses Lisa Alther has tapped:

- *seeing* (shaft of moonlight, pink sand beach, motel overlooking the sea, gray eyes gazing)
- *hearing* (clashing palms, accordion music)
- *taste* (baklava oozing honey)

With a little imagination we might also include the sense of *touch* if we can acknowledge that gray eyes gazing into hers across the Nullarbor Plain might be touching her in a figurative manner. The only sense we miss is the sense of *smell*, and even here, with a dab of additional imagination, we might include it. Think of the Japanese teahouse, and the aromatic odors that often emanate from it. Spicy, exotic smells are usually in the air, and if we combine their appeal with the moonlight on the futon, we have a strong image-maker. The author doesn't talk about odors, but she refers to something which usually has odors around it, and with sense appeal the hint may often be enough. We think of a Japanese teahouse, and what usually comes to mind?

Spicy aroma. Then, maybe, the quiet people inside and the pillows and the gentility.

But first it's the *smells*.

It isn't necessary, always, to be direct with sense appeal, we can get a similar effect with an indirect reference. For example, we can write about the moldy, dark walls of a prison cell, and while our sense of sight would tell us what we saw, our sense of smell would also react because dark, moldy prison walls have a sour, fetid stench. So it isn't necessary to write about the sourness of the odor; mentioning the existence of the moldy prison walls should be enough, and along with what we see, the image is clearly developed.

Hinting at sense appeal does work. How about these?

- smoking, sparking engine . . . (we know what we see and smell, but don't we hear it too?)
- heavily panting dog . . . (we know what we hear, but don't we also feel the hot breath, and perhaps smell it?)
- shelf of thick, bursting fresh sausage . . . (we know what we taste, but can't we also smell?)

It's the vividness of our portrayal that allows us to hint at certain sense appeal, and we have to be careful that we don't assume more than is there. For example, if we write of a "thick, creamy mushroom soup . . ." our sense of taste is activated, but our sense of smell wouldn't be because mushrooms in a soup don't give off much of an odor. It's not the same as referring to garlic, for instance, where taste and smell and even touch would come into play. We have to think in vivid terms and be prepared to pull in the actual sense reference if we are in doubt. Hinting is fine, so long as we're *sure*.

On the other hand, an accomplished writer doesn't need to hint where he or she can portray events clearly and limitlessly. A direct appeal to the senses provides the most dramatic method for developing imagery and setting a scene. Take a look at the way T. Coraghessan Boyle does it in his novel, *Budding Prospects,* about growing marijuana in the high, unpopulated forests in northern California. The narrator and his friends are trying to develop a huge marijuana farm, and they plant thousands of seedlings in plastic cups and put them on shelves in a ramshackle building they call the "nursery." They hope the seedlings will germinate there and then they will replant them in the ground. The narrator acts as general security for the farm and tends to farm repairs while the others mostly come and go. The narrator notices that during the night many seedlings are being destroyed, and he vows to find out how and why.

I was puzzled, distressed. I'd watched the infinitesimal green filaments emerge from the earth, crooked as sweetly as dollar signs, and then come back the following morning to see they'd been grazed to the root as I slept. Night after night I stalked the greenhouse, sitting in darkness, breath suspended, ears perked, waiting for the telltale crunch of mandibles or the scurry of soleless feet, and always I'd been skunked. There was nothing there—neither beetles, nor aphids. Nor snails, leafhoppers, fruit flies or flying sheep for that matter. Just a silence, a silence so absolute I could hear the seeds rupturing their shells . . .

Here we have an appeal to the senses of hearing and sight, the narrator listening for sounds that would tell him who and what was attacking the tiny plants, as he watched the sprouts and saw they had been destroyed by morning. What makes the appeal so vivid is the author's use of descriptive words and phrases along with his reference to hearing and seeing, so we get strong images. He writes of "green filaments" . . . "dollar signs" . . . ; he has the plants "grazed" while he "stalked" . . . he tried to hear the "crunch of mandibles" and the "scurry of soleless feet" . . . and he could hear "the seeds rupturing . . ."

He's used nouns, adjectives, verbs to paint his images, and their vivid effect is what makes the sense appeal work. He could have written that he waited to hear the noise of the insects chewing, instead of the "crunch of mandibles." Or he could have written that he watched the little green buds stick out of the earth, instead of the "infinitesimal green filaments emerge . . ." The same meaning applies; the reader wouldn't be confused about what he meant. But would the same word-picture develop?

Put it another way: would we *hear* the "noise of the insects chewing," if these were the words on the page? It is our senses, remember, that we're trying to excite, and flat words and phrases don't accomplish that well. The better choice, of course, is to heighten the vividness of the prose and to refer to the "crunch of mandibles" because it carries more drama and because it sparks an image. We *must* spark that image.

So the author doesn't speak of the plants cut to their roots; he refers to them as being "grazed," and we get an image of something chewing them off. The narrator doesn't speak of himself walking around the nursery night after night, he writes that he "stalked . . . ," and we get an image of someone storming about, angry, watchful, tireless. Now the word-picture forms.

And we are involved. That's what an appeal to the senses is trying to accomplish, to involve the reader in the story by exciting one or more of his or her senses. Actually, it's a major reason why readers read, as Stanley Schmidt points out:

"Most readers do not pick up a novel or story to admire the author's cleverness in turning a phrase, but to experience vicariously something they cannot experience directly. Your job is to make readers *forget* that they are reading and give them the illusion of *being* in the story, seeing and hearing and smelling and feeling what's happening to your characters."

Appealing to the reader's sense is the way we show rather then tell, but to work, the appeal must be made with some degree of vividness. The important thing is that the reader *wants* his or her senses activated, otherwise they wouldn't be reading in the first place, and as writers we can take comfort in the knowledge that both of us—writer and reader—are seeking the same goal.

So, activate those senses, involve the reader . . .

And watch the drama take hold.

18

Make That Closing "Solid"!

And they lived happily ever after.

The classic ending. We've read it innumerable times in fairy tales and fantasies, and we're cheered by its comfortable, settled image. We won't worry about these characters any longer, we know everything will turn out all right. Happiness is on the horizon, joy and success will come unbidden, and the future is already written.

That's why this is the classic ending. Readers are left with no doubts. There are no overhanging questions, no unresolved dilemmas. *And they lived happily ever after*. The story ends with all loose ends tied.

In a real sense this is what we strive for with every piece of writing. Our ending should leave readers without questions or uncertainties. Remember that readers read to be entertained, and somewhere in there a level of satisfaction must be attained. To be entertained and to *feel* entertained is to find satisfaction. An ending which leaves questions and uncertainties is one which leaves the reader *dissatisfied*. Readers have a right to expect fair treatment from writers, and one expectation is that endings will not bring confusion or guessing games. From the reader's point of view it is the writer who created the field, and it is the writer who should keep it level and clear. Readers are the audience, not the creators, so readers shouldn't be forced into another role, where they decide how the story will end and which loose ends to tie up. Readers *expect* a proper ending, and writers should be prepared to give it to them.

Solid closings are what we're after, a logical final step to the story, a place where questions will be answered and where a final glimpse of the major character or characters will show movement to a defined future. Think of a story as progressing along the rim of a circle; closer and closer it comes to the point where it began, but until it reaches that point its journey isn't finished. A void remains.

So we work to close the circle, and that means bringing the story back to where it began. And we don't close the circle with flimsy threads—we make that closing *solid!*
- the reader must feel he or she has been participating in the work and the ending
- all the reader's major questions have been answered
- matters have been and will continue to proceed along a logical path and to a logical future

Think of *Macbeth*. Shakespeare called it a tragedy, and it certainly is. In the last few scenes the two major characters, Macbeth and Lady Macbeth, die, and it is logical they do so. Shakespeare closed that circle by leaving no loose ends or flimsy uncertainties; the reader is satisfied to see these people dispatched because they *should* have been dispatched.

Now suppose Shakespeare hadn't closed his circle so tightly, suppose Macbeth remains alive and escapes. His kingdom is lost, his wife is dead, and he is a wanted man. But the circle is not closed because he might still mount an army and attempt to reclaim the throne, or his life might gain stature and respectability in exile. In either case his wife's death at the end of the story seems unjustified if Macbeth, who really ignited things in the first place, remains alive. The ending is incomplete, the reader is dissatisfied, and the closing is not solid.

Then, too, the dramatic effect of the ending is reduced. It doesn't seem as exciting, somehow, if Macbeth survives (given his crime of regicide), and this will work on the overall sense of "showing" the reader what is happening. Showing is reduced because the drama itself is dissipated, and story excitement ebbs. With showing less effective, the inclination would be to slip into telling or explaining because the story must continue to move forward, regardless of dramatic effect. It's a principle to remember: *the less solid the closing, the less effective the showing.*

Why is a solid closing so important? Marshall Cook offers one answer: "The conclusion is the second most important part of the [story]. Those last few sentences leave a lingering impression." He was writing about nonfiction here, but the principle applies to fiction, as well. The final sentences tend to stay with us longer than any other portion of the story, and the reason is because it is the last connection the reader has to the writer. When we want to remember that writer, or that story, we usually think of how the story came out, of its ending—"Those last few sentences," in Marshall Cook's words.

And they lived happily ever after. So often, this is what we take away from those fairy tales and fantasies we read (or had read to us) as children; this is what we remember most clearly—*Cinderella, Snow White, The Old Woman Who Lived in a Shoe*—it is the ending we tend to focus upon, and we are satisfied because in stories like these, there's no room for lingering dissatisfaction. We know what to expect, and that's what we get.

Basically, there are two paths to conclusions, linear and circular. When I described the progress of a story following the rim of a circle, I was referring to the latter where the story comes back and meets the beginning. For example, in Evelym Waugh's *Brideshead Revisited*, the narrator begins his tale when, as a soldier during World War Two, he returns to the area of his youth in command of a company of men. Then he digresses and flashes back for the great bulk of the story, only to come back to the point where he began. He has made a complete circle, and at the end must close that circle, which he does by clearing up unanswered questions. When Waugh has his narrator enter the old manor house and reflect on what it has meant to him and many others, he sees its message as a small red flame that

"... burns again for other soldiers, far from home, farther, in heart than Acre or Jerusalem. It could not have been lit but for the builders and the tragedians, and there I found it this morning, burning anew among the old stones."

And so the circle is closed, tying up the loose ends.

The linear path follows a straight line rather than a circle, but even here the close must touch base with the opening to maintain a consistent story line. For example, if the story begins with a mysterious event, the end should not focus on romantic involvement while the mysterious event remains unresolved. There must be consistency all the way through, a step-by-step progression of the story line to a logical conclusion, a goal. It isn't circular because events don't return to where they began, but it must be played out logically. Take a look at Tom Clancy's books where the story proceeds from a perceived danger (missing nuclear submarine, terrorist wrath etc.) to confrontation after confrontation, but always with an eye towards eliminating the danger. This is linear storytelling because characters and circumstances are much changed from the beginning, and while there is resolution of the problem posed at the beginning, everything has been directed towards a goal. Each step in the story has proceeded towards this goal, rather than around in a circle back towards the place where things began. For example, in Clancy's *The Hunt For Red October,* the ending has the defecting submarine finally arrive at its destination, a rendezvous with NATO naval forces and survival for the crew. Had Clancy wished to use a circular route, he would have focused his story on the strong clash of loyalties within the mind of the submarine captain (instead of offering as a given the fact that the captain had made up his mind and that was that!), and then, finally, the captain would have decided his loyalties remained with his native land and he would have returned home. Obviously, this type of ending would not have produced as exciting a book as the one Clancy wrote, yet it would have provided us with a deeper sense of the captain's character and this might have carried its own appeal. The point is that certain stories lend themselves more to the linear path to the ending (mystery-suspense, adventure, romance) because they focus on a *goal.* Other stories seem more suited to the circular (character-dominated, odyssey-like, quest-related) because they get the reader back to where the story has started. There's drama potential in both choices, and the savvy writer must understand which will fit best with the body of the story he or she is writing. In either case, however, the "showing" potential is brought out only if the circle is closed or the linear goal is reached. Otherwise, dramatic effect is reduced because the reader will have questions and uncertainties.

Then there's the hopeful ending: *And they lived happily ever after* . . . The appeal for such a story conclusion is wide and understandable, and many writers are comfortable with it. Both linear as well as circular paths to endings can be hopeful, and no less a writer than Andrew Greeley has risen in defense:

> "I'm not contending that all novels should end with a touch of hope; a writer must be true to his/her vision. I am merely saying that a hopeful ending is as valid as any other . . . The hopeful ending, however, is likely to satisfy most readers precisely because we are creatures who are constrained to hope, even when intellectually we assert we don't want to hope . . ."

The key to making the hopeful ending a solid one lies in the drama we are able to develop. A mushy, inoffensive, directionless ending will have little or any drama, and the story will slowly collapse upon itself. Readers are going to remember little except for a sense of dissatisfaction. But an ending that is packed with drama (read: emotion) will give the reader a jolt and a memory, even if everything comes out all right. Take a look at the way Susan Fromberg Schaeffer ends her novel, *Buffalo Afternoon,* a story of the Viet Nam war and its aftermath among the soldiers who had to cope with post-traumatic stress syndrome because of their return to a hostile America. Pete is the main character, and he goes through a myriad of physical and emotional discomforts. Finally Pete begins the agonizing process of self-healing. Twenty years have now gone by since he returned home, and in the last scene he and his buddy, Sal, are walking in the old neighborhood, and Pete asks Sal if cares about big cars or big television sets:

> "I can afford them," Sal said. "I don't care about them."
>
> "See?" said Pete. "I can't afford them and I don't care about them. We're not Americans."
>
> "Maybe we're new Americans," Sal said.

"I like the sound of that," Pete said. "Yeah, I do."

They walked past the church. "I used to hide in the bushes there," Pete said, pointing. "When it rained, I came out here and scrubbed myself down, naked."

"I know," said Sal.

"It's a good day. It's even a good life. I'm gonna make it," Pete said.

"Yeah," Sal said, smiling. "Now you think so?"

"It's *afternoon,*" Pete said. "It's Buffalo afternoon for us. We're going to make it. It's the peaceful time. It's time to wander the fields and bring it all back home . . ."

The book ends five lines later with moistness in Pete's eyes and a smile on his face, and the reader knows that Pete will now be all right, that he has survived the terror and the agony of his post-Viet Nam emotional somersaulting. What makes the ending a solid one is the emotional outpouring that develops in the last few lines. Pete and Sal wander through the neighborhood, and we get a strong dose of nostalgia as Pete points out the old church where he used to hide in the bushes. Then, we see them both reject standard American values of big cars and big television sets, yet they do their rejecting without anger or confrontation, and that means they aren't trying to prove anything to anyone; they have merely taken a stand and are comfortable with it. Then, they celebrate their knowledge that they will "make" it.

These are strong emotions, and as the characters feel them we feel them, also. The nostalgia, the comfort, the confidence that Pete and Sal show us bring the book to a satisfying—and hopeful—ending, and we can go away feeling good about things.

And they lived happily ever after.

Well, perhaps that's a bit strong. But we take away the sense that Pete and Sal have left the dark days behind, and that's hopeful enough.

And satisfying.

The mood or atmosphere of the ending need not be star-bursts of joy and happiness. The important thing is to appeal to the reader's emotions by developing the emotions of the characters or the situation. The ending is "solid" when the reader can walk away satisfied, and this usually happens when the reader can *feel* what is happening and has no unanswered questions. We might write:

He could feel a light spring to his step as he dodged through the scrub pines, his view ahead unimpeded by the morning shadows that had somehow lifted in the dewy morning light.

THE END

Or we could write:

His body had no spring, no vibrancy, only a rectitude of resolve. He would make it through the forest, but the shadowy pines would not shield his grief. Nothing ever would.

THE END

We have two different moods here, rebirth and resignation. In the first example, the character has worked his way through obstacles to the point where he can see some sort of victory ahead. He is confident and optimistic, and there's every indication that matters will work out to his satisfaction. Here is a hopeful ending that matches the mood of the character, and this is the way it worked out in *Buffalo Afternoon.*

But note the second example. The mood here is anything but optimistic, in fact it reeks of gray, dreary melancholia. Yet, there is hope here, as well. The character, in spite of his somber attitude, knows he'll survive and reach his objective—but that doesn't make him any happier! He's depressed and that's the way things will stand.

Yet the reader is left with hope because the character will survive, and the reader can take away a sense of satisfaction because there won't be any questions about the character's future. The hope is in survival, not unrestrained joy, but for the reader this should be enough. Emotions—both the character's and the reader's—have been touched.

Ernest Hemingway handled hope amidst a background of somberness in the final passages of his *A Farewell To Arms*, his story of a young American officer and a British nurse who fall in love during the First World War in Italy. Catherine, the nurse, becomes pregnant, and Frederick Henry, the officer, deserts his unit to take her to Switzerland where she can have the baby. After an arduous trip they arrive at a Swiss clinic, but Catherine and the baby do not survive the birth. In these final lines Henry has just witnessed Catherine's death, and he runs into the doctor in the clinic hallway. The doctor says:

> "I know there is nothing to say. I cannot to tell you—"
>
> "No," I said. "There's nothing to say."
>
> "Good night," he said, "I cannot take you to your hotel?"
>
> "No, thank you."
>
> "It was the only thing to do," he said, "The operation proved—"
>
> "I do not want to talk about it," I said.
>
> "I would like to take you to your hotel."
>
> "No, thank you."
>
> He went down the hall. I went to the door of the room.
>
> "You can't come in now," one of the nurses said.
>
> "Yes, I can," I said.
>
> "You can't come in yet."
>
> "You get out," I said. "The other one, too."
>
> But after I had got them out and shut the door and turned off the light it wasn't any good. It was like saying good-by to a statue. After a while I went out

and left the hospital and walked back to the hotel in the rain.

Certainly the dialogue here adds drama and helps to create an image of a grief-stricken man attempting to maintain a last thread of connection with his deceased wife. The emotions fly at us: sadness, anger, depression, all of them bundled to offer a word-picture of a somber hospital scene which can involve us and our feelings of empathy for Frederick Henry. We share his grief and his sadness, and we understand that this is an appropriate place to close the story.

Even in the somberness of this time, however, Hemingway offers hope. Frederick Henry has lost his lover and his child, he is an army deserter, and he has come to despise war and all it stands for. In a world where military victory will assure immortality, he has nothing to offer or to grasp . . . except his ability to survive.

And that's the hope that Hemingway provides because Frederick Henry *will* survive. In the final paragraph he has made his peace with Catherine and the baby's death ("It was like saying good-by to a statue"), and he has resumed his place in the world ("After a while I went out and left the hospital and walked back to the hotel in the rain."). Hemingway doesn't allow his character to be consumed by the grief, only to be moved by it, and in this way he allows the reader to feel a satisfaction in Frederick Henry's ultimate survival.

This is a solid closing; it shows emotions, depicts the scene, and allows the reader to be involved in it. Drama and excitement are sure to follow.

Any loose ends? Any unresolved questions?

None that I can see.

Bibliography

Books

Burroway, Janet. *Writing Fiction*. Boston: Little, Brown & Co. 1987.

Curry, Peggy Simpson. *Creating Fiction From Experience*. Boston: The Writer Inc. 1964.

Kilpatrick, James. *The Writer's Art*. New York: Andrews, McMeel & Parker, 1984.

Madden, David. *A Primer of the Novel For Readers and Writers*. Metuchen, New Jersey: Scarecrow Press. 1980.

Sloane, William. *The Craft of Writing*. New York: W.W. Norton and Co. 1979.

Vivante, Arturo. *Writing Fiction*. Boston: The Writer Inc. 1980.

Zinsser, William. *On Writing Well* (4th edition). New York: HarperCollins. 1990.

Articles

Baker, Samm Sinclair. "Three Surefire Ways to Write and Sell Nonfiction." *The Writer*, March, 1989.

Bloom, Pauline. "The Ruffled Blouse Syndrome." *Writer's Digest*, October, 1987.

Blythe, Hal and Sweet, Charlie. "Time Release in Fiction," *Writer's Digest*, May, 1988.

Boyll, Randall. "When They Cry It Makes Us Happy." *Writer's Digest*, May, 1987.

Cook, Marshall. "Seven Steps to Better Manuscripts." *Writer's Digest*, September, 1987.

Creamer, E.S. "Giving Your Fiction the Light Touch." *Writer's Digest*, December, 1988.

Davis, Dorothy Salisbury. "It's Entertainment." *The Writer*, July, 1989.

Friesner, Esther M. "Now What Do We Do With the Alligators?" *Writer's Digest*, January, 1988.

Greeley, Andrew. "In Defense of Hopeful Endings." *Writer's Digest*, January, 1987.

Kress, Nancy. "The Tension of Contrast." *Writer's Digest*, February, 1991.

Madden, David. "How to Craft Compelling Stories." *Writer's Digest*, June, 1990.

Newton, Michael. "How to Bring Your Action/Adventure Novels to Life." *Writer's Digest*, August, 1990.

O'Cork, Shannon. "The Truth, More or Less, As Long As it Makes a Good Story." *Fiction Writer's Market*, 1986.

Schmidt, Stanley. " 'Staging' Your Fiction." *Writer's Digest*, May, 1990.

Schweitzer, Darrel. "Making Your Fiction Three-Dimensional." *Writer's Digest*, December, 1987.

Sheckley, Robert. "Dramatizing Your Fiction." *Writer's Digest*, April, 1989.

Sommer, Elyse. "Sharpen Your Writing With Similes." *Writer's Digest*, August, 1990.

Tapply, William. "What If . . . ?". *The Writer*, January, 1989.

Whitney, Phyllis. "Beginnings." *The Writer*, April, 1989.

Index